C

HYMNS  S

LIST

1992

THE
HYMNS AND SONGS LIST
1992

Compiled by David Barker

Hodder & Stoughton
LONDON   SYDNEY   AUCKLAND

The Table of Sunday Themes and the Tables of Psalms and Readings for Morning and Evening Prayer and for Holy Communion on Sundays are reproduced with permission from *The Alternative Service Book 1980* which is copyright © The Central Board of Finance, The Church of England.

Hymns Ancient and Modern Revised, *100 Hymns for Today*, *More Hymns for Today*, *Hymns Ancient and Modern Abridged* and *Hymns Ancient and Modern New Standard* are listed by kind permission of Hymns Ancient and Modern Limited, St Mary's Works, St Mary's Plain, Norwich, Norfolk, NR3 3BH.

Mission Praise volumes 1 and 2, *Mission Praise Combined Edition*, *Mission Praise Supplement* and *Junior Praise* are listed by kind permission of HarperCollins Publishers Limited, 77–85 Fulham Palace Road, Hammersmith, London W6 8JB.

Hymns and Psalms is listed by kind permission of the Methodist Publishing House, 20 Ivatt Way, Peterborough PE3 7PG.

Songs of Fellowship Books 1–4, *Hymns of Fellowship*, *Songs and Hymns of Fellowship* and *New Songs 1990/91* are listed by kind permission of Kingsway Music Limited, 1 St Anne's Road, Eastbourne, East Sussex BN21 3UN.

British Library Cataloguing in Publication Data
The hymns and songs list 1992.
I. Barker, David
782.27

ISBN 0-340-56511-X

Published by Hodder and Stoughton,
a division of Hodder and Stoughton Ltd,
Mill Road, Dunton Green, Sevenoaks, Kent TN13 2YA
Editorial Office: 47 Bedford Square, London WC1B 3DP

Photoset by SX Composing, Rayleigh, Essex

Printed in Great Britain by Clays Ltd, St. Ives plc.

CONTENTS

INTRODUCTION

Choosing hymns and songs for single worship events is relatively easy – the selection can be made from items which are well known by the congregation, or which will suit a particular occasion. The difficulties tend to arise when selecting material week by week and month by month, as inspiration can begin to wear thin. Christmas and other festival times also present a challenge as there are a large number of additional services to plan.

The Hymns and Songs List was born as an answer to the needs I have described. In 1985 I realised that, in my own church, we were not using the hymn and song books at our disposal to their full potential. I began by creating a handwritten list of hymns and songs for each week of the lectionary year – a good idea, but awkward to use. That list soon gave way to a simplified lectionary hymn list, but based on only two source books.

The Hymns and Songs List 1992 is a carefully chosen selection of hymns and songs from an extensive computer database. The book has been designed to provide a fresh and easy-to-use resource for all who lead public worship, and a new selection will be made available each year.

Using *The Hymns and Songs List*

There is a variety of ways in which *The Hymns and Songs List* can be used in the planning of worship, whether or not the Anglican lectionary is followed.

The simplest method for those using the lectionary consists in looking at the listing for the appropriate lectionary week and choosing the required number of items from the selection provided. For those who do not use the lectionary, material relevant to the theme of a service can be easily identified from the contents pages and the Thematic Index.

The List, however, is primarily intended as a springboard to help develop thought patterns, in looking beyond the obvious and familiar. In my own planning for weekly worship, I use a simple form as shown below. Using the list, I enter items for the appropriate Sunday or theme in the right hand column, and add the titles of any extra items, such as psalms or anthems, which may be appropriate. In the left hand column, I then list the services for the day, by type and with the time for each one, together with the number of items required and a list of others involved in planning the service. It is then a matter of reviewing the hymns and songs listed, and attempting to fit them into the services in order. This method will not always supply a complete answer to the planning of services for each week, but will certainly provide a starting point.

You will notice that we have included a blank column for you to list material from any book which is not already shown. This might include one of the excellent collections of new versions of the Psalms, or one of the new hymn book supplements which have been published recently.

Sunday 12th April 1992 Palm Sunday	**HYMNS/SONGS**
10:00 a.m. Family Service	
Organist/Pianist/Music Group Leader: Minister/Preacher: Prayers/Intercessions:	
Hymn book/song book:	
1) 2) 3) 4) 5)	
6:30 p.m. Communion	
Organist/Pianist/Music Group Leader: Minister/Preacher: Prayers/Intercessions:	
Hymn book/song book:	**ANTHEMS/SOLO ITEMS**
1) 2) 3) 4) 5)	
Communion	**NOTES**
1) 2)	

I would encourage you to keep in touch with the current developments in music for worship and use whatever material is helpful to the congregation you serve. Although so obvious, I also encourage you to pray continually for God's guidance over the selections you make.

I hope that you and your congregation will be helped by this publication, and drawn nearer to the heart of God in your worship.

Hymn and Song Books Included in the List
Hymns Ancient & Modern Revised
Listed under the heading AMR. All hymns listed in this column are from Hymns Ancient & Modern Revised except those with a prefix +.

100 Hymns for Today
Listed in the AMR column and prefixed + between +1 and +100.

More Hymns for Today
Listed in the AMR column and prefixed + between +101 and +200.

Hymns Ancient & Modern Abridged
Most hymns listed in the AMR column without a + prefix appear in Hymns Ancient & Modern Abridged. Table 1 includes a conversion table showing Hymns Ancient & Modern Revised numbers with those used in the Abridged version.

Hymns Ancient & Modern New Standard
Almost all hymns listed in the AMR column appear in Hymns Ancient & Modern New Standard. Table 1 includes a conversion table showing Hymns Ancient & Modern Revised numbers with those used in Hymns Ancient & Modern New Standard.

Mission Praise Volume 1 (Mission England Praise)
These are listed in the second column MP and are the hymns with numbers between 1 and 282.

Mission Praise Volume 2
Listed in the MP column as hymns with numbers between 283 and 647.

Mission Praise Supplement
Listed in the MP column as hymns with numbers between 648 and 758.

Mission Praise Combined Edition
All songs in the MP column as numbers or stars *** are in the Combined Edition. Table 5 can be used to convert these numbers to those used in the Combined Edition.

Junior Praise
All hymns in the JP column.

Hymns for Today's Church
All hymns in the HTC column.

Church Family Worship
All hymns in the CFW column.

Hymns and Psalms
All hymns in the H&P column.

Songs and Hymns of Fellowship (All Volumes)
The column marked SOF and Tables 3 & 4 contain all the information required to use any combination of books within the Songs and Hymns of Fellowship range as follows:

Songs of Fellowship Books 1, 2 and 3 and Hymns of Fellowship
These are listed in the SOF column by the number used in the combined Songs and Hymns of Fellowship volume. Table 3 is a conversion chart showing those numbers with the individual music or word book numbers.

Songs of Fellowship Book 4
All songs from Book 4 are listed in the SOF column and indicated by the symbol 4/ in front of the number.

New Songs 1990/91
Songs from the Songs of Fellowship New Songs 1990/91 Book are listed in the SOF column and indicated by the number 90/91. Table 4 contains an index for the New Songs 1990/91 book.

Hymn Titles
The wording of hymns has changed much over the years, especially with the introduction of hymn books in modern language. Because of this, some of the hymn titles may vary from those you are used to. For example "Thou, whose almighty word" and "God, whose almighty word" are the same hymn. In The Hymns and Songs List titles are generally taken from the first hymn book in which they appear. Some hymns have therefore appeared by older titles whilst others are listed by their more modern title.

It is worth remembering to check with the hymn book you use after selection of the hymns to ensure that the correct title is written down on your service order.

Where different themes are set for Year 1 and Year 2, the hymns have been combined. It is usually easy to select the titles suitable for the current year's theme.

ACKNOWLEDGMENTS

There are so many people who have had to put up with my continual questions, jokes and absent-mindedness that it would be very difficult to name them all here. There are those, however, who deserve special mention at the beginning of this book:

Derek Wooldridge, the Rector of St Paul's Church in York, without whom my walk with God would have been a different story altogether. Thank you for challenging, supporting and correcting me when necessary.

Chris, Joy, Simon and Peter Cullwick, Church leader and friends at St Andrew's. Thank you for allowing me freedom to lead our worship in the direction I felt God was taking us, for giving me the space to work, and just for being there.

The musicians and singers at St Andrew's. Thank you for your patience and long suffering. So often I speak too loudly, quickly, and with so much enthusiasm that you do a marvellous job keeping up with me!

Liz and Mick Fryer, for believing in The Hymns and Songs List even when I wasn't sure that anybody but me would use it.

The congregation at St Andrew's, who have been, and continue to be my guinea-pigs week by week. Thank you for your support and the example you set in living a life that connects with reality, loving God first and giving him the glory.

Finally, to Liz, my wife and best friend, and to Andrew, the wonderful son God has given to us. Thank you for suffering the long hours spent sorting through hymns, the days when you couldn't see the floor for hymn books, and for putting up with my singing.

To God be the glory!
Great things he hath done!
So loved he the world
that he gave us his Son.

To God be the glory!
For ever and ever.

Amen.

LECTIONARY WEEKS

9 before Christmas: *the Creation*

	AMR	MP	JP	HTC	CFW	H&P	SOF	other
All creatures of our God and King	172	287		13	283	329		
All people that on earth do dwell	166	6	4	14	367	1	8	
All things bright and beautiful	442	298	6	283	266	330		
Almighty Sovereign Lord							4/6	
Angel voices, ever singing	246	304		307		484	15	
At the name of Jesus	225	15	13	172	305	74	26	
Come, rejoice before your maker				17	96			
Creator of the earth and skies	+18			320		419		
Father, you're enthroned							4/24	
Fill your hearts with joy and gladness		353		30	513			
For the beauty of the earth	171	356	48	298	182	333		
For the fruits of his creation	+124	52		286	522	342		
From before the earth's foundation							119	
From the sun's rising		666					4/26	
God of concrete, God of steel	+33							
God that madest earth and heaven	26					641		
God the Father of creation				427	277			
God who made the earth			63					
God who spoke in the beginning	+135							
God, whose farm is all creation	+37		61	282		344		
Great is thy faithfulness		62	64	260	523	66	143	
He made the stars to shine			76					
Holy, holy, holy, Lord God Almighty	160	73		7	329	7	168	
How great thou art		173	179				407	
I will give you praise		696					255	
I'll praise my maker		427		20		439		
If I were a butterfly			94		273			
Immortal, invisible	372	103		21	267	9	210	
Jesus is Lord		119	137	s17	286	260	278	
Let us with a gladsome mind	377	471	154	23	280	27	324	
Lord, how majestic you are							90/91	
Lord of creation, to you be all praise		479				699		

	AMR	MP	JP	HTC	CFW	H&P	SOF	other
Love divine	205	149		217	387	267	353	
Morning has broken		***	166	265	279	635		
My God, how wonderful you are	169	498		369	341	51	370	
My God is so big, so strong			169		82			
Not the grandeur of the mountains					382			
O God my creator							397	
O Lord of every shining constellation	+78			314				
O Lord of heaven and earth and sea	480			287	498	337		
O Lord our God (We will magnify)		512					409	
O Lord, our Lord		727					4/129	
O praise ye the Lord	376	519		354	490		421	
O worship the King	167	178		24	351	28	428	
Praise the Lord, you heavens	368			583	284	15		
Praise to the Lord, the Almighty	382	192		40	89	16	452	
Sing a new song to the Lord		203		349	420	57		
Songs of praise the angels sang	369			350		512		
Stand up, clap hands			225		274			
The earth is the Lord's		748						
The earth is yours, O God				290	514			
The earth was dark until you spoke		288			447			
The Lord reigns, let the earth rejoice							524	
The works of the Lord are created				26				
Think of a world without any flowers			254		276	572		
We believe in God Almighty				10	613			
We believe in God the Father		611					4/173	
We really want to thank you, Lord		256	268		494		587	
When morning gilds the skies	223	266	278	223		276	603	
Who put the colours in the rainbow			288		518			
Who's the king of the jungle			289					
With wonder, Lord, we see your works	+198				271	353		
Worthy, O worthy		636			296		624	
Yes, God is good – in earth and sky		640	293			363		
You make my heart feel glad							90/91	

8 before Christmas: the Fall

	AMR	MP	JP	HTC	CFW	H&P	SOF	other
Amazing grace		10	8	28	158	215	10	
And can it be		11		588	389	216	12	

	AMR	MP	JP	HTC	CFW	H&P	SOF	other
Father God in heaven				358	171			
Father of heaven, whose love profound	164			359		519		
God who created this Eden of earth	+36							
He was pierced		684					4/39	
In Adam we have all been one	+141					420		
Jesus is a friend of mine			136		165			
Jesus is King, and I will extol		449			169		277	
Jesus shall reign where'er the sun	220	123		516	415	239	289	
Joy to the world, the Lord has come		708		197	664	77	4/88	
Judge eternal, throned in splendour		***		329	62	409		
Just as I am	349	132	146	440	411	697	304	
King of glory, King of peace	367	462			157	499		
Lord, as I wake I turn to you	+152			267	162	634		
Lord Jesus, think on me	200			316		533		
Lord, teach us how to pray aright	317			367	173	551		
Nature with open volume stands	+164					174		
O lift us up, strong son of God						427		
O Lord, our guardian and our guide	300			374	124			
O Lord, the clouds are gathering		728					4/130	
O what a mystery I see		725					4/137	
Open our eyes, Lord		181			612		420	
Out of the depths I cry to thee	322					429		
Praise to the holiest	185	191		140		231	450	
Rekindle your first love							4/143	
Restless souls, why do you scatter	364			443				
Safe in the shadow of the Lord		549		445	395			
Seek ye first		201	215		168	138	471	
Speak, Lord, in the stillness		562		253	174			
Spirit divine, inspire our prayers	239	563		240	309	327		
Take, eat, this is my body		570					493	
The God who rules this earth	+92							
The Lord is King! Lift up your voice	175	226		183	290	58	519	
The Lord made man, the scriptures tell				143				
The Lord will come, and not be slow	52					245		
There is no moment of my life					164	428		
Walking in a garden	+185							
We turn to you, O God	+189					412		

	AMR	MP	JP	HTC	CFW	H&P	SOF	other
What a friend we have in Jesus		262	273	373	179	559	598	
What Adam's disobedience cost	+191					430		
What shall I do my God to love						46		
When all your mercies, O my God	177	***		39	383	573		
Wonderful Counsellor, Jesus					641			
Would Jesus have the sinner die?						185		

7 before Christmas: *the Election of God's People: Abraham*

	AMR	MP	JP	HTC	CFW	H&P	SOF	other
Abba, Father, let me be		1	2		399		1	
All the way, all the way		296			207			
Be thou my vision	+10	17		545		378	38	
Children of the heavenly King	295			566	556			
El-Shaddai, El-Shaddai		341					4/19	
Father, hear the prayer we offer	182	43	41	360	85	436		
Father of Jesus Christ						693		
For God so loved the world					402			
From before the earth's foundation							119	
God is working his purpose out	271	373	57	188		769	134	
God of light and life's creation				561	505			
Guide me, O thou great Jehovah	296	63		528	129	437	144	
I am trusting you, Lord Jesus		81	86	433	406		183	
I believe in God the Father				434	404			
I bind myself to God today	162			5		695		
If my people, who bear my name		697					4/50	
Let every Christian pray	+145			230		305		
Like a mighty river flowing		145		32	407			
Lord, all-knowing, you have found me					394			
Lord God, thou art our maker	+56							
Lord Jesus Christ, you have come to us	+58	480	156	417	390	617	342	
My Lord, I did not choose you				107				
O come, and let us to the Lord						567		
O happy band of pilgrims	289			530				
O thou who camest from above	329	174		552		745	424	
One shall tell another		531			30		417	
Put thou thy trust in God	310							
Reign in me, sovereign Lord		546			403		4/142	
Salvation is found in no-one else					397			

	AMR	MP	JP	HTC	CFW	H&P	SOF	other
So I've made up my mind					143			
The God of Abraham praise	631	581		9		452	507	
The light of Christ		223		8				
Through the night of doubt	292			466	128	441		
To God be the glory		248	259	584	412	463	559	
We are a chosen people		607					565	
We are your people: Lord	+186							
We come unto our fathers' God		614				453		
What a wonderful saviour is Jesus			274		567			

6 before Christmas: the Promise of Redemption: Moses

	AMR	MP	JP	HTC	CFW	H&P	SOF	other
All my hope on God is founded	+3	292		451		63		
Alleluia! Sing to Jesus	399	67		170		592	151	
Bind us together, Lord		21	17	s4	119		39	
Bread of heaven, on you we feed	411			398				
Break thou the bread of life		316				467	46	
Captain of Israel's host						62		
Children of the heavenly King	295			566	356			
Christ is made the sure foundation		27		559	483	485	54	
Come ye faithful, raise the anthem	222	***		205		813		
For I'm building a people of power		50	47		469		109	
Glorious things of thee are spoken	257	59		494	183	817	123	
Happy are they	261			473	125	711		
He was pierced		684					4/39	
Here he comes, robed in majesty					57			
How did Moses cross the Red Sea			83					
How good a thing it is				497	116			
I have made a covenant							195	
In Christ there is no east or west	+43	435		322	429	758		
In my life, Lord, be glorified		105			495		216	
Jesus the joy of loving hearts		128		413			296	
Jesus, we enthrone you		131					343	
Lead us, heavenly Father, lead us	311	465		525	111	68	306	
Let there be love shared among us		137			58		318	
Let us with a gladsome mind	377	471	154	23	280	27	324	
Lord, enthroned in heavenly splendour	400	476		416		616	336	
Moses, I know you're the man						450		

	AMR	MP	JP	HTC	CFW	H&P	SOF	other
Now thank we all our God	379	163	175	33	199	566	386	
O bread to pilgrims given						620		
O Lord, our guardian and our guide	300			374	124			
Only by grace can we enter							90/91	
Revive your church O Lord	362	198		515	479	780	465	
Spirit of God most high				242	480			
Spirit of the living God, move				s24	318			
The Lord has led forth his people		741			121		518	
There is a land of pure delight	285			575		822		
Through all the changing scenes	290	246		46	576	73		
Thy hand, O God, has guided	256	247	298	536	130	784		
We are one body in the Lord					120			
We have come into this house		253		s29	117		581	
You shall go out with joy		281			118		641	

5 before Christmas: *the Remnant of Israel*

	AMR	MP	JP	HTC	CFW	H&P	SOF	other
A safe stronghold our God is still	183	284		523		661	17	
At the name of Jesus	225	15	13	172	305	74	26	
At your feet we fall		308			251		28	
Christ is surely coming		323			598			
City of God, how broad	258					809		
City of God, Jerusalem				187	595			
Dear Lord and Father of mankind	184	40	37	356		673	76	
Eternal Father, strong to save	487	340		285	350	379		
Fling wide the gates					291			
God is the refuge of his saints						53		
Great shepherd of your people	247			363		490		
Guide me, O thou great Jehovah	296	63		528	129	437	144	
He is Lord, he is Lord		69	75	s7	586	256	159	
I have made a covenant							195	
I'm not ashamed to own my Lord		100		448		677		
If my people, who bear my name		697					4/50	
Jesus, where'er thy people meet	245			371		549		
Lead us, heavenly Father, lead us	311	465		525	111	68	306	
Let the desert sing				198				
Lighten our darkness now the day				278	593			
My Lord, he is a-coming soon					588			

	AMR	MP	JP	HTC	CFW	H&P	SOF	other
O bless the God of Israel					585			
O come, O come, Emmanuel	49	506	177	66		85		
O God, our help in ages past	165	503		37	50	358		
O Jesus, I have promised	331	172		531		704	400	
O thou not made with hands	259					656		
Oft in danger, oft in woe	291	524		524	530	715		
Open, Lord, my inward ear						540		
Out of the depths I cry to thee	322					429		
Praise him, praise him, Jesus		186	203		304		439	
Rejoice, the Lord is King	216	195		180	301	243	463	
Restore, O Lord, the honour		196			589		464	
Sing to God new songs of worship		560		352	249			
Tell me, why do you weep					590			
The church's one foundation	255	217		501		515	505	
The God of Abraham praise	631	581		9		452	507	
Through all the changing scenes	290	246		46	576	73		
Through the night of doubt	292			466	128	441		
Thy hand, O God, has guided	256	247	298	536	130	784		
When Israel was in Egypt's land			276					

Advent 1: the Advent Hope

	AMR	MP	JP	HTC	CFW	H&P	SOF	other
And art thou come with us to dwell						415		
Awake, awake, O Zion		309					29	
Behold the darkness		12					34	
Christ is surely coming		323			598			
Christ is the world's light	+107			321		455		
Christ is the world's true light	+13			323		456		
Come and see the shining hope		33		191	578			
Come, thou long-expected Jesus	54	335				81		
Darkness like a shroud		658					4/17	
For unto us a child is born		359					113	
God is working his purpose out	271	373	57	188		769	134	
Hail to the Lord's anointed	219	64		190		125	146	
Hark the glad sound	53	385	68	193	580	82		
He is Lord, he is Lord		69	75	s7	586	256	159	
Hills of the north rejoice	269					237		
How lovely on the mountains		79	84		421		176	

	AMR	MP	JP	HTC	CFW	H&P	SOF	other
I cannot tell		83		194		238	185	
Jesus comes with all his grace						168		
Jesus, hope of every nation				58				
Jesus, King of kings							4/80	
Jesus, my Lord, how rich thy grace	+48					147		
Jesus shall reign where'er the sun	220	123		516	415	239	289	
Lift up your heads to the coming King		473			208		328	
Lift up your heads, you mighty gates	+150					240		
Lion of Judah							330	
Lo, he comes with clouds descending	51	141		196	599	241	332	
Make way, make way for Christ		491			587		4/119	
Mine eyes have seen the glory						242	368	
My Lord, he is a-coming soon					588			
O come, O come, Emmanuel	49	506	177	66		85		
On Jordan's bank the Baptist's cry	50	528	186		581	84		
Prepare the way for Jesus to return							457	
Prepare the way of the Lord							458	
Sing a new song to the Lord		203		349	420	57		
Sing we the King		206	218			244		
Soldiers of Christ, arise	303	207		533	529	719	483	
Tell me, why do you weep					590			
The advent of our King	48							
The Lord will come, and not be slow	52					245		
Therefore the redeemed		593					531	
Thy kingdom come, O God	262			334	67	783		
Thy kingdom come; on bended knee	263							
What a wonderful saviour is Jesus			274		567			
When he comes we'll see just a child		625					599	
When the King shall come again				200	594			
When the Lord in glory comes		628	280	201				

Advent 2: the Word of God in the Old Testament

	AMR	MP	JP	HTC	CFW	H&P	SOF	other
All hail the power of Jesus' name	217	5		587		252	7	
All scriptures are given					608			
At thy feet, O Christ, we lay	6					630		
Begin my tongue, some heavenly theme						2		
Break now the bread of life		316			614	467	46	

	AMR	MP	JP	HTC	CFW	H&P	SOF	other
Come, divine interpreter						468		
Come, Holy Ghost, our hearts inspire	+115					469		
El-Shaddai, El-Shaddai		341					4/19	
Father of mercies, in your word	251			247	601			
From all that dwell below the skies	630			580	419	489	118	
God has spoken – by his prophets				248		64		
God has spoken to his people		367		s11	611		130	
God speaks, and all things come to be						23		
God, who hast caused to be written	+134					472		
God whose almighty word	266	244		506	416	29		
Hark the glad sound	53	385	68	193	580	82		
Help us, O Lord, to learn	+40			493	615	474		
How firm a foundation		76		430				
How sure the scriptures are				249				
I give you all the honour		412					191	
I have made a covenant							195	
Jesus, hope of every nation				58				
Jesus – the name high over all		126		213		264	294	
Let God speak							311	
Long ago prophets knew	+151					83		
Lord, be thy word my rule	327			250				
Lord, I have made thy word my choice	+157					475		
Lord, thy word abideth	250	486		251	620	476		
O what a mystery I see		725					4/137	
O word of God incarnate		177				478		
Open your eyes		729					4/134	
Seek ye the Lord		202					472	
Teach me your way, O Lord							4/155	
Thanks to God whose word was spoken	+90			255	621	483		
The heavens declare your glory, Lord	252			254		481		
The Lord will come, and not be slow	52					245		
The prophets spoke in days of old	+180							
The will of God to mark my way					607			
We believe in God Almighty				10	613			
Wide, wide as the ocean			292		357			

Advent 3: the Forerunner

	AMR	MP	JP	HTC	CFW	H&P	SOF	other
Alleluia, alleluia, give thanks		9	3	s3	252	250	5	
Awake, awake, fling off the night	+9							
Christ is the world's true light	+13			321		456		
Christ, whose glory fills the skies	7	320		266	134	457		
City of God, Jerusalem				187	595			
Clear the road, make wide the way							4/13	
Fill thou my life	373	48		541		792	104	
For unto us a child is born		359					113	
From all that dwell below the skies	630			580	419	489	118	
Give me joy in my heart	+126			s11	446	492		
Give me oil in my lamp		58	50					
Go forth and tell		61		505	506	770		
Go, tell it on the mountain		672	65		424	135		
God forgave my sins (Freely, freely)		60	54	s12	293		126	
God has exalted him					294		129	
God is love: let heaven adore him	+32	371			368	36		
God's Spirit is in my heart					422	315		
How gracious are their feet						449		
How great is God Almighty					313			
How lovely on the mountains		79	84		421		176	
In Christ there is no east or west	+43	435		322	429	758		
Jesus put this song into our hearts		457			423		4/81	
Let all the world in every corner	375	135		342	49	10		
Lift up your heads to the coming King		473			208		328	
Lo, from the desert homes	552							
Lo, he comes with clouds descending	51	141		196	599	241	332	
Love divine	205	149		217	387	267	353	
Make way, make way for Christ		491			587		4/119	
O for a thousand tongues	196	168		219		744	394	
On Jordan's bank the Baptist's cry	50	528	186		581	84		
Prepare the way for Jesus to return							457	
Prepare the way of the Lord							458	
Rejoice in the Lord always		194	208				462	
Rejoice, the Lord is King	216	195		180	301	243	463	
Sing a new song to the Lord		203		349	420	57		
The day you gave us, Lord, is ended	33	218	236	280	436	648	506	
The earth was dark		288			447			
We have a gospel to proclaim	+98	617		519	433	465		

	AMR	MP	JP	HTC	CFW	H&P	SOF	other
What a friend we have in Jesus		262	273	373	179	559	598	
When he comes we'll see just a child		625					599	

Advent 4: *the Annunciation*

	AMR	MP	JP	HTC	CFW	H&P	SOF	other
A messenger named Gabriel				73				
Angels from the realms of glory	64	302	10	77	661	92		
Away in a manger		310	12	72	651	94		
Blest are the pure in heart	335	313		110		724		
Come and sing the Christmas story				81	638			
Come, thou long-expected Jesus	54	335				81		
Earth was waiting				54				
Emmanuel, Emmanuel		659			642		79	
For Mary, mother of our Lord	+27							
For unto us a child is born		359					113	
God is working his purpose out	271	373	57	188		769	134	
God of glory, we exalt your name		376			337		136	
Her virgin eyes saw God incarnate born	513							
How sweet the name of Jesus sounds	192	78		211		257	178	
I've found it hard, Lord							237	
Immanuel, O Immanuel		699					4/57	
It came upon the midnight clear	66	442	116	87		108		
Jesus Christ the Lord is born			131	83	671			
Jesus, good above all other	+45			96	195	732		
Jesus, name above all names		122	141		226		288	
Joy to the world, the Lord has come		708		197	664	77	4/88	
Judge eternal, throned in splendour		***		329	62	409		
Let it be to me		711					4/94	
Little donkey, little donkey					644			
Long ago, prophets knew	+151					83		
Long time ago in Bethlehem					645			
Look to the skies		717			657			
Lord, enthroned in heavenly splendour	400	476		416		616	336	
Lord, now let your servant					98			
Lord, you were rich		***		63	673			
Majesty – worship his majesty		151	160		339		358	
Mary sang a song, a song of love					643			

	AMR	MP	JP	HTC	CFW	H&P	SOF	other
My soul doth magnify							379	
My soul doth magnify the Lord		159					380	
Name of all majesty		499		218	306			
O come, O come, Emmanuel	49	506	177	66		85		
O little town of Bethlehem	65	509	182	88	647	113		
O what a mystery I see		725					4/137	
O worship the Lord in the beauty	77	179		344	92	505	429	
Once in royal David's city	432	530	185	67	646	114		
Royal sons of a royal King							470	
See him lying on a bed of straw		553	214	91	656	118		
Songs of praise the angels sang	369			350		512		
Tell out, my soul	+89	215	229	42	187	86	498	
The angel Gabriel from heaven came						87		
The God whom earth and sea and sky	512							
The light of Christ		223			8			
The virgin Mary had a baby boy			251	s25	655			
The wise may bring their learning			253		105			
There is singing in the desert					133			
This child, secretly comes		743						
Thou didst leave thy throne	363	237			108	154	552	
When he comes we'll see just a child		625					599	
While shepherds watched	62	629	285	94	658	120		
Worthy, O worthy		636			296		624	
You are the King of glory		279	296		221		630	

Christmas Eve: the Birth of Christ

	AMR	MP	JP	HTC	CFW	H&P	SOF	other
All the way, all the way		296			207			
Angels from the realms of glory	64	302	10	77	661	92		
At this time of giving		651					4/8	
Away in a manger		310	12	72	651	94		
Blest are the pure in heart	335	313		110		724	40	
Born in the night, Mary's child		315				95		
Christians awake! Salute	61	325		78		96		
Come and hear the joyful singing					662			
Come and sing the Christmas story				81	638			
Come watch with us		***						
Cradle rocking, cattle lowing					649			

	AMR	MP	JP	HTC	CFW	H&P	SOF	other
Ding-dong! Merrily on high		336	38		667			
Emmanuel, Emmanuel		659			642		79	
Father, never was love so near		663						
For unto us a child is born		665						
Girls and boys, leave your toys					668			
Glad music fills the Christmas sky				82				
Glory be to God in heaven		364		581	24			
God of glory, we exalt your name		376			337		136	
Good Christians all, rejoice		379		85		191		
Happy Christmas, everybody					639			
Hark! The herald angels sing	60	384	69	59	660	106		
His name is higher than any other		71			640		163	
Holy child, how still you lie		683		60	653			
In the bleak mid-winter	67	437				107		
Infant holy, infant lowly		439	110	86				
It came upon the midnight clear	66	442	116	87		108		
Jesus Christ the Lord is born			131	83	671			
Jesus, name above all names		122	141		226		288	
Joy to the world, the Lord has come		708		197	664	77	4/88	
Like a candle flame		712						
Little donkey, little donkey					644			
Long time ago in Bethlehem					645			
Love came down at Christmas				62		105		
Mary had a baby, yes, Lord					650			
Now dawns the Sun of righteousness		722						
O come, all ye faithful	59	504	176	65	672	110		
O little town of Bethlehem	65	509	182	88	647	113		
O Prince of peace				89				
On Christmas night all Christians sing		***				115		
On the eve of Christmas						116		
Once in royal David's city	432	530	185	67	646	114		
Peace to you		730					4/138	
Ring out the bells					665			
See, amid the winter's snow		552	213	90		117		
See him lying on a bed of straw		553	214	91	656	118		
Silent night, holy night		558	219	95	648	112		
Songs of praise the angels sang	369			350		512		
The first nowell the angel did say		580	238	93	109	119		
The light of Christ		223			8			

	AMR	MP	JP	HTC	CFW	H&P	SOF	other
The people who walked in darkness	80			71				
The virgin Mary had a baby boy			251	s25	655			
The wise may bring their learning			253		105			
This child, secretly comes		743						
Thou didst leave thy throne	363	237			108	154	552	
Tonight (Glory to God)		745						
When shepherds watched					659			
While shepherds watched	62	629	285	94	658	120		
Within a crib my saviour lay				70				
You are the King of glory		279	296		221		630	

Christmas Day

	AMR	MP	JP	HTC	CFW	H&P	SOF	other
A great and mighty wonder	68			49		90		
A song was heard at Christmas				75				
Angels from the realms of glory	64	302	10	77	661	92		
At this time of giving		651					4/8	
Away in a manger		310	12	72	651	94		
Behold the amazing gift of love						666		
Born in the night, Mary's child		315				95		
Child in the manger		657		51	652			
Child of the stable's secret birth				53		124		
Christ is born within a stable					666			
Christians awake! Salute	61	325		78		96		
Come and hear the joyful singing					662			
Come and join the celebration		326			669	97		
Come and sing the Christmas story				81	638			
Cradle rocking, cattle lowing					649			
Ding-dong! Merrily on high		336	38		667			
Emmanuel, Emmanuel		659			642		79	
Emmanuel, (Emmanuel)		342						
For unto us a child is born		359					113	
For unto us a child is born		665						
Girls and boys, leave your toys					668			
Glad music fills the Christmas sky				82				
Glory be to God on high						101		
God rest you merry, gentlemen				84		103		
Good Christians all, rejoice		379		85		104		

	AMR	MP	JP	HTC	CFW	H&P	SOF	other
Happy Christmas, everybody					639			
Hark! The herald angels sing	60	384	69	59	660	106		
Holy child, how still you lie		683		60	653			
In the bleak mid-winter	67	437				107		
Infant holy, Infant lowly		439	110	86				
Isn't he beautiful?		441					228	
It came upon the midnight clear	66	442	116	87		108		
Jesus, name above all names		122	141		226		288	
Joy to the world, the Lord has come		708		197	664	77	4/88	
Like a candle flame		712						
Little donkey, little donkey					644			
Long time ago in Bethlehem					645			
Lord, you were rich		***		63	673			
Love came down at Christmas		489		62		105		
Mary sang a song, a song of love					643			
O come, all ye faithful	59	504	176	65	672	110		
O come and join the dance		723						
O little town of Bethlehem	65	509	182	88	647	113		
Once in royal David's city	432	530	185	67	646	114		
Peace to you		730					4/138	
Ring out the bells					665			
See, amid the winter's snow		552	213	90		117		
See him lying on a bed of straw		553	214	91	656	118		
Silent night, holy night		558	219	95	648	112		
Sing lullaby! Lullaby baby				92				
The first nowell the angel did say		580	238	93	109	119		
The light of Christ		223			8			
The virgin Mary had a baby boy			251	s25	655			
This child, secretly comes		743						
Unto us a boy is born		606	263			127		
What child is this		624						
When things began to happen				69				
While shepherds watched	62	629	285	94	658	120		
You are the King of glory		279	296		221		630	
You are the mighty King		642					632	

Christmas 1: (1) the Incarnation
(2) the Presentation

	AMR	MP	JP	HTC	CFW	H&P	SOF	other
A great and mighty wonder	68			49		90		
A song was heard at Christmas				75				
All the way, all the way		296			207			
Angels from the realms of glory	64	302	10	77	661	92		
Away in a manger		310	12	72	651	94		
Bethlehem, what greater city	76				93			
Born in the night, Mary's child		315				95		
Child of the stable's secret birth				53		124		
Christmas for God's holy people				79				
Come and hear the joyful singing					662			
Come, let us worship the Christ				207				
Come, rejoice before your maker				17	96			
Darkness like a shroud		658					4/17	
Earth was waiting				54				
Emmanuel, Emmanuel		659			642		79	
Faithful vigil ended	+120	660		55	562			
From heaven you came		361			449		120	
Glory be to God in heaven		364		581	24			
God from on high hath heard	63					102		
God of glory, we exalt your name		376			337		136	
God rest you merry, gentlemen				84		103		
Had he not loved us				57				
Hail to the Lord who comes	544					126		
He is born, our Lord and Saviour		676						
His name is higher than any other		71			640		163	
I'll be still and know			93					
Jesus Christ the Lord is born			131	83	671			
Jesus, good above all other	+45			96	195	732		
Jesus, hope of every nation				58				
Joy to the world, the Lord has come		708		197	664	77	4/88	
Long ago prophets knew	+151					83		
Long time ago in Bethlehem					645			
Lord Jesus Christ, you have come to us	+58	480	156	417	390	617	342	
Lord, you were rich		***		63	673			
Love came down at Christmas				62		105		
Mary sang a song, a song of love					643			

	AMR	MP	JP	HTC	CFW	H&P	SOF	other
Now dawns the Sun of righteousness		722						
O bless the God of Israel					585			
O come and join the dance		723						
O worship the Lord in the beauty	77	179		344	92	505	429	
Once in royal David's city	432	530	185	67	646	114		
Praise to the holiest	185	191		140		231	450	
Ring out the bells					665			
Shepherds came				74	670			
Sing a song, a joyful song					654			
Son of God, eternal Saviour	207			102				
Take my life, and let it be	361	212		554	151	705	496	
Tell out, my soul	+89	215	229	42	187	86	498	
The first nowell the angel did say		580	238	93	109	119		
The light of Christ		223			8			
The wise may bring their learning			253		105			
Thou didst leave thy throne	363	237			108	154	552	
To us a child of royal birth	71			64				
When the Lord came to our land					100			
Where is this stupendous stranger	+194							
While shepherds watched	62	629	285	94	658	120		
Wonderful Counsellor, Jesus					641			
Word of the Father everlasting					101			
Worthy, O worthy		636			296		624	
You are the King of glory		279	296		221		630	

Christmas 2: (1) the Holy Family
(2) the Light of the World

	AMR	MP	JP	HTC	CFW	H&P	SOF	other
Angels from the realms of glory	64	302	10	77	661	92		
As with gladness men of old	79	305	9	99	104	121		
Behold the darkness		12					34	
Born in the night, Mary's child		315			95			
Christ is the world's light	+107			321		455		
Come and praise the Lord our King			34	s8	188			
Crown him with many crowns	224	39		174	198	225	75	
El-Shaddai, El-Shaddai		341					4/19	
Faithful vigil ended	+120	660		55	562			
Father God in heaven					358	171		
Father, we adore you		44	44	s5	191		96	

	AMR	MP	JP	HTC	CFW	H&P	SOF	other
For the beauty of the earth	171	356	48	298	182	333		
Glory to God in the highest		365	51					
Hail to the Lord's anointed	219	64		190		125	146	
Holy child, how still you lie		683		60	653			
I heard the voice of Jesus say	351	85				136	196	
Jesus Christ the Lord is born			131	83	671			
Jesus, good above all other	+45			96	195	732		
Jesus put this song into our hearts		457			423		4/81	
Like a candle flame		712						
Lord, now let your servant					98			
Lord of all hopefulness	+61		157	101	86	552		
Lord of the home	+161					367		
Now dawns the Sun of righteousness		722						
Now thank we all our God	379	163	175	33	199	566	386	
O come and join the dance		723						
O worship the Lord in the beauty	77	179		344	92	505	429	
Once in royal David's city	432	530	185	67	646	114		
One shall tell another		531			30		417	
Shepherds came				74	670			
The heavenly child in stature grows	78							
The wise may bring their learning			253		105			
There is singing in the desert					133			
This child, secretly comes		743						
Thou didst leave thy throne	363	237			108	154	552	
We three kings of Orient are		622	271		99			
We were not there to see you come				121				
What child is this		624						
Wise men, they came				100				
Worthy, O worthy		636			296		624	

Epiphany 1: *Revelation: the Baptism of Jesus*

	AMR	MP	JP	HTC	CFW	H&P	SOF	other
Amazing grace		10	8	28	158	215	10	
Awake, awake, fling off the night	+9							
Behold the servant of the Lord						788		
Bethlehem, what greater city	76				93			
Born of the water				382				

	AMR	MP	JP	HTC	CFW	H&P	SOF	other
Christ, when for us you were baptised	+109					129		
Come, let us join our cheerful songs	221	37		206	555	810	64	
Come, Lord, to our souls come down	+15					470		
Come, rejoice before your maker				17	96			
God moves in a mysterious way	101	375				65	135	
God of glory, we exalt your name		376			337		136	
Guide me, O thou great Jehovah	296	63		528	129	437	144	
Hail to the Lord's anointed	219	64		190		125	146	
Holy Spirit, ever dwelling						303		
I bind myself to God today		477		437		423		
I know not why God's wondrous grace							200	
I'm saved by the grace of God							212	
In Christ there is no east or west	+43	435		322	429	758		
Jesus, Jesus Christ in majesty							283	
Jesus – the name high over all		126		213		264	294	
Lord, now let your servant					98			
Now is eternal life	+69					203		
O for a thousand tongues	196	168		219		744	394	
O love, how deep, how broad	187					229		
O Spirit of the living God				513		322		
Praise and thanksgiving	+173					350		
Royal sons of a royal King							470	
Songs of thankfulness and praise	81			98				
Spirit divine, inspire our prayers	239	563		240	309	327		
Spirit of God, descend upon my heart						313		
The wise may bring their learning			253		105			
There is singing in the desert					133			
Thou didst leave thy throne	363	237			108	154	552	
To the name of our salvation	190			222		80		
We are a kingdom							565	
When Jesus came to Jordan	+193					132		
When the Lord came to our land					100			
Word of the Father everlasting					101			
Worthy, O worthy		636			296		624	
You are the King of glory		279	296		221		630	

Epiphany 2: *Revelation: the First Disciples*

	AMR	MP	JP	HTC	CFW	H&P	SOF	other
All people that on earth do dwell	166	6	4	14	367	1	8	
Before Jehovah's awesome throne	370			15		61		
Big man standing by the blue waterside			16					
Blessed is the man					138			
Christ in me is to live					140			
Christ, whose glory fills the skies	7	320		266	134	457		
Day by day, dear Lord						671		
Dear Lord and Father of mankind	184	40	37	356		673	76	
Dear Master, in whose life I see						522		
Firmly I believe and truly	186			429	145			
From heaven you came		361			449		120	
God's Spirit is in my heart					422	315		
I am trusting you, Lord Jesus		81	86	433	406		183	
I want to be part of your army							4/63	
I want to walk with Jesus Christ		444	124	s16	141			
I will make you fishers of men			123					
If you want to be great					142			
Jesus calls us, o'er the tumult	533	116		104		141		
Jesus, where'er thy people meet	245			371		549		
Lead us, heavenly Father, lead us	311	465		525	111	68	306	
Lord Jesus, once you spoke to men	+59			112				
Loving shepherd of your sheep	444			305	147			
Master, speak! Thy servant heareth		155				535	362	
My faithful shepherd is the Lord					560			
My Lord, I did not choose you				107				
Now thank we all our God	379	163	175	33	199	566	386	
O Jesus, I have promised	331	172		531		704	400	
One who is all unfit to count						539		
Seek ye first		201	215		168	138	471	
Send me out from here, Lord		556			425			
So I've made up my mind					143			
Take up your cross	333			114				
Teach me, O Lord, thy holy way						748		
Tell me the stories of Jesus		573	228			153		
The journey of life					210			
The Lord my shepherd rules my life				45	137			
To him we come		602		518	152			

	AMR	MP	JP	HTC	CFW	H&P	SOF	other
We are your people: Lord	+186							
When I survey	108	265	277	147	238	180	602	
Who does Jesus love					144			

Epiphany 3: *Revelation: Signs of Glory*

	AMR	MP	JP	HTC	CFW	H&P	SOF	other
A boy gave to Jesus			1					
Almighty Sovereign Lord							4/6	
Be still, for the presence		652					4/10	
Bind us together, Lord		21	17	s4	119		39	
Bread of heaven, on you we feed	411			398				
Break now the bread of life		316			614	467	46	
Children of the heavenly king	295			566	356			
Christ is the heavenly food	+106							
Come, sing praises to the Lord above					115			
For I'm building a people of power		50	47		469		109	
Glorious things of thee are spoken	257	59		494	183	817	123	
God is our strength and refuge		372		527	77			
God of concrete, God of steel	+33							
Guide me, O thou great Jehovah	296	63		528	129	437	144	
Holy, holy, holy, Lord God Almighty	160	73		7	329	7	168	
How glorious Zion's courts appear						448		
I am the God that healeth thee							4/46	
I cannot count your blessings, Lord		692					4/49	
I cannot tell		83		194		238	185	
I hunger and I thirst	413			409		730		
I will give thanks to thee		98					254	
I'm expecting great things of you							206	
Jesus, where'er thy people meet	245			371		549		
Lord, how majestic you are							90/91	
Love divine	205	149		217	387	267	353	
My Lord is higher than a mountain			170					
O Lord our God (We will magnify)		512					409	
O thou not made with hands	259					656		
Peter and James and John in a sailboat			197					
Peter and John went to pray		199	198					
Praise to the Lord, the Almighty	382	192		40	89	16	452	
Show your power, O Lord		734					4/148	

	AMR	MP	JP	HTC	CFW	H&P	SOF	other
Sing to God new songs of worship		560		352	249			
Spirit of the living God, move				s24	318			
That mighty resurrection word						658		
The brightness of God's glory				221				
The earth is the Lord's		748						
The Lord has led forth his people		741			121		518	
The Spirit of the Lord		746					4/164	
Thy hand, O God, has guided	256	247	298	536	130	784		
To God be the glory		248	259	584	412	463	559	
We have come into this house		253		s29	117		581	
Who took fish and bread			286					
With Jesus in the boat we can smile			291					
Yours, Lord, is the greatness		647					643	

Epiphany 4: *Revelation: the New Temple*

	AMR	MP	JP	HTC	CFW	H&P	SOF	other
Behold the temple of the Lord						808		
Bind us together, Lord		21	17	s4	119		39	
Blessed city, heavenly Salem	474					485		
Burn, Holy Fire							49	
Christ is made the sure foundation		27		559	483	485	54	
Christ is our corner-stone	243			564	482			
Church of God, elect and glorious				504	444			
Come and praise the living God		327					59	
Come, my soul, thy suit prepare	319					546		
For I'm building a people of power		50	47		469		109	
Glorious things of thee are spoken	257	59		494	183	817	123	
God is building a house		369						
God is in his temple						494		
Guide me, O thou great Jehovah	296	63		528	129	437	144	
He who dwells		679						
Here he comes, robed in majesty					57			
How glorious Zion's courts appear						448		
How lovely is thy dwelling-place		399						
How lovely is thy dwelling-place		685					175	
I have built in my people a temple							193	
I stand before the presence		422					229	
In my life, Lord, be glorified		105			495		216	

	AMR	MP	JP	HTC	CFW	H&P	SOF	other
Jerusalem, my happy home	282			569				
Jerusalem on high				565				
Jesus, where'er thy people meet	245			371		549		
Lead us, heavenly Father, lead us	311	465		525	111	68	306	
Let earth and heaven agree						226		
Let there be love shared among us		137			58		318	
Let there be singing							319	
Let us praise God together			152	s18	438			
Lord of the worlds above	248							
Lord, you need no house				546				
Love divine	205	149		217	387	267		
My heart overflows		494					371	
One there is above all others		532				149		
Praise the Lord, praise him							4/140	
The church's one foundation	255	217		501		515	505	
The promised land							529	
Then I saw a new heaven		589						
Therefore the redeemed of the Lord		593					531	
Through the night of doubt	292			466	128	441		
We have come into this house		253		s29	117		581	
Where high the heavenly temple stands	204			184				
With joy we meditate the grace	+197	***				235		
You shall go out with joy		281			118		641	

Epiphany 5: *Revelation: the Wisdom of God*

	AMR	MP	JP	HTC	CFW	H&P	SOF	other
All my hope on God is founded	+3	292		451		63		
All scriptures are given					608			
Almighty Father of all things						375		
And can it be		11		588	389	216	12	
Be thou my vision	+10	17		545		378		
Can man by searching find out God	+105			426		76		
Come, workers for the Lord	+17					380		
Father of mercies, in your word	251			247	601			
Father, Son, and Holy Ghost						791		
Fill thou my life	373	48		541		792	104	
From you all skill and science flow	479			310		389		
God has spoken to his people		367		s11	611		130	

	AMR	MP	JP	HTC	CFW	H&P	SOF	other
God moves in a mysterious way	181	375				65	135	
God whose almighty word	266	244		506	416	29		
Hark, what a sound						236		
Help us, O Lord, to learn	+40			493	615	474		
Immortal, invisible	372	103		21	267	9	210	
Jesus' hands were kind hands			134			393		
Jesus shall reign where'er the sun	220	123		516	415	239	289	
King of glory, King of peace	367	462			157	499		
Lord of light, whose name shines						796		
Lord, speak to me that I may speak		148		510	428	553		
Lord, teach us how to pray aright	317			367	173	551		
Lord, thy word abideth	250	486		251	620	476		
Nature with open volume stands	+164					174		
New every morning is the love	4	161	171	270		636		
O Lord of every shining constellation	+78			314				
Open our eyes, Lord		181			612		420	
Praise to the holiest	185	191		140		231	450	
Put thou thy trust in God	310							
Reap me the earth	+174					623		
Servant of all, to toil for man						383		
Thanks to God whose word was spoken	+90			255	621	483		
The spacious firmament on high	170					339		
The will of God to mark my way					607			
This day God gives me	+183							
We believe in God Almighty				10	613			
Wide, wide as the ocean			292		357			
With wonder, Lord, we see your works	+198				271	353		
Your way, not mine, O Lord				555				

Epiphany 6: *Revelation: Parables*

	AMR	MP	JP	HTC	CFW	H&P	SOF	other
As pants the hart for cooling streams	314					416		
Behold, the mountain of the Lord						50		
Behold the servant of the Lord						788		
Blessed is the man					138			
Christ, whose glory fills the skies	7	320		266	134	457		
Come, let us with our Lord arise	+166				375	575		

	AMR	MP	JP	HTC	CFW	H&P	SOF	other
Father of mercies, in your word	251			247	601			
Firmly I believe and truly	186			429	145			
From the rising of the sun		54	49		139		121	
God has spoken – by his prophets				248		64		
Great is our redeeming Lord						438		
Happy are they	261			473	125	711		
How pleased and blest was I						497		
How sure the scriptures are				249				
I want to walk with Jesus Christ		444	124	s16	141			
If you want to be great					142			
Light of gladness				277	154			
Lord Jesus, once you spoke to men	+59			112				
Lord, make your word my rule				250				
Loving shepherd of your sheep	444			305	147			
Not far beyond the sea	+68					477		
O God of truth, whose living word	309							
O send thy light forth						537		
Praise him, praise him, Jesus		186	203		304		439	
Rise and hear, the Lord is speaking	+176							
Seek ye first		201	215		168	138	471	
Shepherd divine, our wants relieve	318					558		
So I've made up my mind					143			
Strengthen for service	+88			423		626		
Thanks to God whose word was spoken	+90			255	621	483		
The day of resurrection	132			161		208		
The heavens declare your glory		598		254		481		
The journey of life					210			
The prophets spoke in days of old	+180							
This is the day, this is the day		239	255	s28	319	578	547	
To him we come		602		518	152			
Wake, O wake				199		249		
When Jesus walked upon this earth				317				
Where cross the crowded ways of life						431		
Who does Jesus love					144			

9 before Easter: *Christ the Teacher*

	AMR	MP	JP	HTC	CFW	H&P	SOF	other
Almighty God, thy word is cast						466		
Can man by searching find out God	+105			426		76		
Christ be my leader						709		
Come, all who look to Christ today						765		
Come to us, creative Spirit				308		377		
Father of mercies, in your word	251			247	601			
Firmly I believe and truly	186			429	145			
God speaks, and all things come to be						23		
God's Spirit is in my heart					422	315		
I am trusting you, Lord Jesus		81	86	433	406		183	
I heard the voice of Jesus say	351	85				136	196	
If you want to be great					142			
Jesus, my truth, my way						734		
Jesus the Lord said, 'I am the bread'		458				137		
Jesus, the word bestow						768		
Lord, if at thy command						771		
Lord Jesus, once you spoke to men	+59			112				
Lord, teach me how to pray aright	317			367	173	551		
Lord, that I might learn of thee						737		
O changeless Christ for ever new				108				
O Jesus, I have promised	331	172		531		704	400	
Praise him, praise him, everybody			201	s21	379	565		
Praise, my soul, the King of heaven	365	187	204	38	459	13		
Praise to the Lord, the Almighty	382	192		40	89	16	452	
Praise we now the word of grace	+84							
Praise you, Lord, for the wonder		541						
Seek ye first		201	215		168	138	471	
Show us your way						133		
Take my life, and let it be	361	212		554	151	705	496	
Teach me thy way, O Lord		569						
Tell his praise in song and story				41				
Tell me the old, old story		572	227			232		
The journey of life					210			
The prophets spoke in days of old	+180							
The voice of God goes out						140		
To him we come		602		518	152			
When I survey	108	265	227	147	238	180	602	
When Jesus walked upon the earth				317				

	AMR	MP	JP	HTC	CFW	H&P	SOF	other
You are the way	199	605		113		234		
Your words to me are life						482		

8 before Easter: *Christ the Healer*

	AMR	MP	JP	HTC	CFW	H&P	SOF	other
A man there lived in Galilee	+1							
A new commandment		283		s26	445			
As pants the hart for cooling streams	314					416		
Be still and know		16	22				37	
Be still, for the presence		652					4/10	
Bread of heaven	411			398				
Come, let us sing of a wonderful love		35	29			691	67	
Dear Lord and Father of mankind	184	40	37	356		673	76	
Father, sending your anointed		351						
Father, we adore you, you've drawn us		352					97	
For the healing of the nations	+28					402		
From you all skill and science flow	479			310		389		
God of mercy, God of grace	264			293	527			
He that is in us is greater		388					4/37	
He was pierced		684					4/39	
Heal me, hands of Jesus				319				
Heal us, Immanuel!						390		
Healing God, Almighty Father		391						
Here, Lord, we take the broken bread				404		604		
How precious, O Lord		400					177	
How sweet the name of Jesus sounds	192	78		211		257	178	
I am the God that healeth thee							4/46	
Immortal love, for ever full	208	***		105		392		
It's your blood		701					4/62	
Jesus' hands were kind hands			134			393		
Jesus put this song into our hearts		457			423		4/81	
Jesus, thy far-extended fame						148		
Just as I am	349	132	146	440	411	697	304	
Lamb of God, Holy One							4/93	
Live, live, live . . . Jesus is living			153					
Lord, come and heal your church		716					4/101	
Lord, have mercy on us							4/102	
Lord, I will celebrate your love							4/107	

	AMR	MP	JP	HTC	CFW	H&P	SOF	other
Lord Jesus, think on me	200			316		533		
Lord, we ask that you would								4/111
Lord, we long for you		713						4/113
Make me a channel of your peace		153	161	s19	470	776		
May the mind of Christ		157	165	550	452	739		
Now thank we all our God	379	163	175	33	199	566	386	
O Christ the healer						395		
O for a thousand tongues	196	168		219		744	394	
O let the Son of God enfold you		508					403	
O thou, whom once they flocked						150		
Peter and John went to pray		199	198					
Praise, my soul, the King of heaven	365	187	204	38	459	13	441	
Rejoice! Rejoice! Christ is in you		543			538		461	
See, Christ was wounded				137				
The voice of God goes out						140		
When all your mercies, O my God	177	***		39	383	573		
With joy we meditate the grace	+197					235		

7 before Easter: *Christ the Friend of Sinners*

	AMR	MP	JP	HTC	CFW	H&P	SOF	other
A purple robe, a crown of thorns				122				
All ye who seek for sure relief	104							
Almighty God, our heavenly Father		650					4/4	
Amazing grace		10	8	28	158	215	10	
And can it be		11		588	389	216	12	
Be thou my vision	+10	17		545		378		
But ye are washed							50	
Christians, seek not yet repose	308			355				
Cleanse me, O God							4/12	
Come, let us sing of a wonderful love		35	29			691	67	
Dear Lord and Father of mankind	184	40	37	356		673	66	
Eternal Father, strong to save	487	340		285	350	379		
Father, hear the prayer we offer	182	43	41	360	85	436		
Father of Jesus Christ						693		
Forgive our sins as we forgive	+29			111		134		
God is love: let heaven adore him	+32	371			386	36		
God is the refuge of his saints						53		
Great is thy faithfulness		62	64	260	523	66	143	

	AMR	MP	JP	HTC	CFW	H&P	SOF	other
He paid a debt he did not owe			77					
He was pierced		684					4/39	
Hear my cry, O God		392						
How can we sing with joy to God				362				
How sweet the name of Jesus sounds	192	78		211		257	178	
I get so excited, Lord, ev'ry time		410					189	
I heard the voice of Jesus say	351	85				136	196	
I stand amazed in the presence		421						
I worship you, O Lamb of God							4/75	
I'm going to say my prayers					167			
I'm special because God has loved me		431	106					
It's your blood		701					4/62	
Jesus, good above all other	+45			96	195	732		
Jesus is a friend of mine		136			165			
Jesus, lover of my soul	193	120		438		528	286	
Just as I am	349	132	146	440	411	697	304	
Lift up your hearts	341			366		405		
Lord God, your love has called us	+156			480		500		
Lord, I was blind		477		437		423		
Lord of all hopefulness	+61		157	101	86	552		
Lord, teach us how to pray aright	317			367	173	551		
May the grace of Christ our saviour	636			370	504	762		
My Lord, I did not choose you				107				
Now thank we all our God	379	163	175	33	199	566	386	
O Jesus, I have promised	331	172		531		704	400	
O sacred head, surrounded	111	521		139		176		
O sinner man, where will you run to			194					
Oh, the joy of your forgiveness		724					4/127	
Only by grace can we enter							90/91	
Seek ye first		201	215		168	138	471	
Spirit divine, inspire our prayers	239	563		240	309	327		
Tell me the stories of Jesus		573	228			153		
The kingdom of God is justice and joy		582		333		139		
There's a way back to God		234	248					
Thou didst leave thy throne	363	237			108	154	552	
What a friend we have in Jesus		262	273	373	179	559	598	
When all your mercies, O my God	177	***		39	383	573		
With joy we meditate the grace	+197	***				235		

Lent 1: the King and the Kingdom: Temptation

	AMR	MP	JP	HTC	CFW	H&P	SOF	other
A safe stronghold our God is still	183	284		523		661	17	
And can it be		11		588	389	216	12	
At the name of Jesus	225	15	13	172	305	74	26	
Awake, our souls; away, our fears	+103					663		
Christian, dost thou see them	91							
Father God in heaven				358	171			
Father, hear the prayer we offer	182	43	41	360	85	436		
Father, lead me day by day			43			790		
Forty days and forty nights	92	360		103		130		
Go, tell it on the mountain		672	65		424	135		
God is good – we sing and shout it		370	55		377		131	
He walked where I walk		678					4/38	
I need thee every hour		92				524		
I'm going to say my prayers					167			
Jesus is a friend of mine			136		165			
Jesus – the name high over all		126		213		264	294	
Join all the glorious names		461		214		78	301	
King of glory, King of peace	367	462			157	499		'
Lead us, heavenly Father, lead us	311	465		525	111	68	306	
Lift up your hearts	341			366		405		
Lord, as I wake I turn to you	+152			267	162	634		
Lord Christ, when first thou cam'st	+54							
Lord Jesus, think on me	200			316		533		
Lord of our life	253	484		529				
Lord, who throughout these forty						131		
O breath of life, come sweeping		164		237	464	777	388	
O Lord, our guardian and our guide	300			374	124			
Open our eyes, Lord		181			612		420	
Praise God today					180			
Safe in the shadow of the Lord		549		445	395			
Seek ye first		201	215		168	138	471	
Shepherd divine, our wants relieve	318					558		
Soldiers of Christ, arise	303	207		533	529	719	483	
Spirit divine, inspire our prayers	239	563		240	309	327		
Spirit of wisdom, turn our eyes						385		
There is no moment of my life					164	428		
We sing the praise of him who died	215			146		182	590	
When all your mercies, O my God	177	***		39	383	573		

	AMR	MP	JP	HTC	CFW	H&P	SOF	other
Where high the heavenly temple stands	204			184				
With joy we meditate the grace	197	***				235		

Lent 2: the King and the Kingdom: Conflict

	AMR	MP	JP	HTC	CFW	H&P	SOF	other
A safe stronghold our God is still	183	284		523		661	17	
Arm of the Lord, awake						433		
Be bold, be strong		312	14		542		4/9	
Behold the amazing gift of love						666		
Christian, dost thou see them	91							
Christian soldiers, onward go				524	530			
Earth, rejoice, our Lord is King						811		
Fight the good fight	304	49		526	546	710	103	
For all the saints	527	51		567	550	814		
For the Lord is marching on							4/25	
For this purpose was the Son of God							111	
God is our fortress and our rock				523				
God is our strength and refuge		372		527	77			
Here from all nations				571	577			
How firm a foundation		76		430				
I danced in the morning	+42		91					
Judge eternal, throned in splendour		***		329	62	409		
Let God arise		467			534		309	
My Lord, you wore no royal crown				118				
Oft in danger, oft in woe	291	524		524	530	715		
Onward, Christian soldiers	629	***		532	551	718	419	
Put on the sword of the Spirit					541			
Rejoice! Rejoice! Christ is in you		543			538		461	
Rise up, O men of God	+85							
Sing my tongue, the glorious battle	97			142		177		
So we're marching along					543			
Soldiers of Christ, arise	303	207		533	529	719	483	
Soldiers of the cross arise	305			534				
Soldiers who are Christ's below	524							
Stand up, stand up for Jesus	307	211	226	535		721	489	
Strong in Christ					547			
Take up your cross	333			114				
Thanks be to God, who gives us		577			539			

	AMR	MP	JP	HTC	CFW	H&P	SOF	other
The head that once was crowned	218	220		182	287	209	508	
The Lord is King, he is mighty		742			537		520	
Through our God we shall do valiantly		600			540		555	
Thy hand, O God, has guided	256	247	298	536	130	784		
Thy kingdom come; on bended knee	263							
Who honours courage here				537				
Who is on the Lord's side		274	287			722	610	

Lent 3: *the King and the Kingdom: Suffering*

	AMR	MP	JP	HTC	CFW	H&P	SOF	other
A man there lived in Galilee	+1							
Bind us together, Lord		21	17	s4	119		39	
Can man by searching find out God	+105			426		76		
Christ is made the sure foundation		27		559	483	485	54	
Come and see, come and see		***					90/91	
Father, hear the prayer we offer	182	43	41	360	85	436		
Father, never was love so near		663						
Father of mercies, in your word	251			247	601			
For I'm building a people of power		50	47		469		109	
For this purpose		358			255		110	
Great shepherd of your people	247			363		490		
Hail, our once-rejected Jesus		383		175		222	145	
Happy are they	261			473	125	711		
He was pierced		684					4/39	
Help us to help each other, Lord	+41			540	439			
Here he comes, robed in majesty					57			
Here is love							4/35	
I stand before the presence		422					229	
In Christ there is no east or west	+43	435		322	429	758		
It's your blood		701					4/62	
Jesus our Lord, our King and our God	+49							
Let us praise God together			152	s18	438			
Light has dawned		719					4/100	
Lord Christ, we praise your sacrifice	+154			132		532		
My Lord, what love is this		***					90/91	
My song is love unknown	102	160		136	215	173	378	
New every morning is the love	4	161	171	270		636		

	AMR	MP	JP	HTC	CFW	H&P	SOF	other
Now join we, to praise our creator	+167					348		
O God of Bethel	299					442		
O love that will not let me go	359	171		486		685	415	
Restless souls, why do you scatter	364			443				
Rock of ages	210	197		444			469	
Such love, pure as the whitest snow		735					4/152	
Take up your cross	333			114				
The hands of Christ				141				
The head that once was crowned	218	220		182	287	209	508	
The price is paid		587			233		528	
Thy hand, O God, has guided	256	247	298	536	130	784		
Victim divine, thy grace we claim						629		
We are one body in the Lord					120			
We sing the praise of him who died	215	258		146		182	590	
When I needed a neighbour	+100		275					
Who can sound the depths of sorrow		754					4/182	
You shall go out with joy		281			118		641	
Your way, not mine, O Lord	356			555				

Lent 4: the King and the Kingdom: Transfiguration

	AMR	MP	JP	HTC	CFW	H&P	SOF	other
Almighty God, we bring you praise		299					9	
Blest are the pure in heart	335	313		110		724	40	
Christ is the world's true light	+13			323		456		
Christ upon the mountain peak	+108			115		155		
Christ, whose glory fills the skies	7	320		266	134	457		
Come and praise the Lord our King			34	s8	188			
Eternal light, eternal light				454		458		
Father, we adore you		44	44	s5	191		96	
Father, we thank you	+24					561		
Firmly I believe and truly	186			429	145			
For he is seated on his Father's throne							107	
From glory to glory advancing	417							
From the rising of the sun		54	49		149		121	
Glorious things of thee are spoken	257	59		494	183	817	123	
Her virgin eyes saw God incarnate born	513							
I am trusting you, Lord Jesus		81	86	433	406		183	
I come with joy to meet my Lord	+140			408	16	610		

	AMR	MP	JP	HTC	CFW	H&P	SOF	other
If you want to be great					142			
Jesus, you are changing me		459					297	
Light of gladness				277	154			
Light's abode, celestial Salem	279							
Lo, God is here! Let us adore	249					531		
Lord, as we rise	+52							
Lord of all hopefulness	+61		157	101	86	552		
Lord, teach us how to pray aright	317			367	173	551		
Lord, you give to us						368		
Love divine	205	149		217	387	267	353	
Meekness and majesty		493					4/122	
My God, how wonderful you are	169	498		369	341	51	370	
O God in heaven, whose loving plan	+74					369		
O Lord of heaven and earth and sea	480			287	498	337		
Once on a mountain top						157		
Our saviour Christ once knelt				116				
Out of the darkness let light shine				447				
Stay, Master, stay						158		
Take my life, and let it be	361	212		554	151	705	496	
The God of Abraham praise	631	581		9		452	507	
The journey of life					210			
Think of a world without any flowers			254		276	572		
Thy kingdom come, O God	262			334	67	783		
Turn the hearts of the children					190			
When I survey	108	265	277	147	238	180	602	
When Jesus led his chosen three				117				
Where the Spirit of the Lord is							606	
With glorious clouds encompassed						184		

Lent 5: *the King and the Kingdom: the Victory of the Cross*

	AMR	MP	JP	HTC	CFW	H&P	SOF	other
All hail the Lamb		648					4/1	
Alleluia, my Father		66			224		149	
Beneath the cross of Jesus		20				165	36	
Bring a psalm							48	
Come on and celebrate		330					69	
Crown him with many crowns	224	39		174	198	255	75	
From heaven you came		361			449		120	

	AMR	MP	JP	HTC	CFW	H&P	SOF	other
Give thanks with a grateful heart		***					4/27	
He gave his life in perfect love		387		405	34			
Here is love							4/35	
In the cross of Christ I glory		107			231	167		
In the name of Jesus		109	111				218	
It is a thing most wonderful	435	110	117	131	232	224		
Lift high the cross	633	139		508		170		
Lift Jesus higher		472					326	
Look ye saints, the sight		475		179		201	334	
Lord Christ, we praise your sacrifice	+154			132		532		
Man of sorrows		154		130	237	228	361	
Meekness and majesty		493					4/122	
My Lord, what love is this		***					90/91	
My song is love unknown	102	160		136	215	173	378	
O dearest Lord, thy sacred head	436			134		172		
O Lord, the clouds are gathering		728					4/130	
O sacred head, surrounded	111	521		139		176		
O what a mystery I see		725					4/137	
Oh the love that drew salvation's plan			181					
On Calvary's tree			183		227			
Once, only once, and once for all	398							
Out of the depths I cry to thee	322					429		
Salvation is found in no-one else					397			
Saviour, and can it be						541		
See, Christ was wounded				137				
Take up your cross	333			114				
The church of God is moving							503	
The hands of Christ				141				
The price is paid		587			233		528	
There is a redeemer		590			228		534	
Victory is on our lips		252					562	
Worthy is the Lamb		280			45		621	
You are crowned with many crowns							4/188	

Palm Sunday: the Way of the Cross

	AMR	MP	JP	HTC	CFW	H&P	SOF	other
A purple robe, a crown of thorns				122				
All for Jesus, all for Jesus				469		251		

	AMR	MP	JP	HTC	CFW	H&P	SOF	other
All glory, laud and honour	98	289		120	202	160		
All the way, all the way		296			207			
At the name of Jesus	225	15	13	172	305	74	26	
Children of Jerusalem		***	24			163		
Clap your hands, all you people		26						
Clear the road, make wide the way							4/13	
Fling wide the gates					291			
Give me joy in my heart	+126			s11	446	492		
Give me oil in my lamp		58	50					
Glory be to Jesus	107			126			125	
Glory, glory in the highest		668					4/29	
Here he comes, robed in majesty					57			
Hosanna, hosanna		682					4/42	
Jesus Christ our great Redeemer		706					270	
Jesus comes with all his grace						168		
Jesus died for all the children			132					
Jesus is a friend of mine			136		165			
Jesus is Lord		119	137	s17	286	260	278	
King forever							4/91	
King of kings and Lord of lords		463	148				305	
Lift high the cross	633	139		508		170		
Lift up your heads to the coming King		473			208		328	
Majesty – worship his majesty		151	160		339		358	
Make way, make way for Christ		491			587		4/119	
Name of all majesty		499		218	306			
O Jesus my King							401	
O the bitter shame and sorrow		523		487		538		
Peter feared the cross	+81							
Prepare the way of the Lord							458	
Ride on, Jesus, all-victorious						272		
Ride on, ride on	99	547	209	119	218	159		
Ride on triumphantly	599							
See him come (His body was broken)							4/145	
Shout for joy to the Lord							475	
Swing wide the gates		733					4/154	
The glory of our King was seen						161		
The royal banners forward go	96					179		
To mock your reign, O dearest Lord	+184							
Trotting, trotting through Jerusalem						162		

	AMR	MP	JP	HTC	CFW	H&P	SOF	other
We cry hosanna, Lord		615			209			
We have a King who rides a donkey			264					
You are the King of glory		279	296		211		630	
You laid aside your majesty		644					638	

Good Friday

	AMR	MP	JP	HTC	CFW	H&P	SOF	other
Ah, holy Jesus				123		164		
All you that pass by		***						
Alleluia, my Father		66			224		149	
Cleanse me from my sin, Lord		30	27		225			
Come and see, come and see		***					90/91	
Father, never was love so near		663						
From heaven you came		361			449		120	
He gave his life in perfect love		387		405	34			
He paid a debt			77					
He was pierced		684					4/39	
Here is love							4/35	
I met you at the cross			103					
I stand amazed in the presence		421						
Immanuel, O Immanuel		699					4/57	
In the cross of Christ I glory		107			231	167		
It is a thing most wonderful	435	110	117	131	232	224		
It's your blood		701					4/62	
Lamb of God, Holy One							4/93	
Lamb of God, whose dying love						550		
Lift Jesus higher		472					326	
Man of sorrows		154		130	237	228	361	
Meekness and majesty		493					4/122	
My Lord, what love is this		***					90/91	
My song is love unknown	102	160		136	215	173	378	
No weight of gold or silver				138	223			
O crucified redeemer	+71					424		
O dearest Lord, thy sacred head	436			134		172		
O my Saviour, lifted	360	518						
O sacred head, surrounded	111	521		139		176		
Oh the love that drew salvation's plan			181					
On Calvary's tree			183		227			

	AMR	MP	JP	HTC	CFW	H&P	SOF	other
Saviour! Thy dying love		551						
Such love, pure as the whitest snow		735					4/152	
Thank you for the cross		739					4/156	
The love of Christ who died for me		***						
There is a green hill far away	214	230	245	148	219	178	532	
There is a redeemer		590			228		534	
Were you there when they crucified	+190		269			181		
When I survey	108	265	277	147	238	180	602	
Who can sound the depths of sorrow		754					4/182	
Worthy is the Lamb		280			45		621	

Easter Day: the Resurrection of Christ

	AMR	MP	JP	HTC	CFW	H&P	SOF	other
All creatures join to say				150	259			
All creatures of our God and King	172	287		13	283	329		
All hail the Lamb		648					4/1	
All heaven declares		649					4/2	
Alleluia, alleluia, give thanks		9	3	s3	252	250	5	
Almighty God, we bring you praise		299					9	
At the Lamb's high feast	139							
At the name of Jesus	225	15	13	172	305	74	26	
At your feet we fall		308			251		28	
Because he died and is risen					568			
Bless the Lord, O my soul		24	19	80			43	
By the working (He is alive)							51	
Christ is alive! Let Christians sing						190		
Christ is risen! Hallelujah		322						
Christ is risen! Hallelujah							4/11	
Christ the Lord is risen again	136	324		153	258	192		
Come, let us with our Lord arise	+116			375		575		
Come on and celebrate		330					69	
Come ye faithful, raise the strain	133			160		194		
Comes Mary to the grave				152				
Crown him with many crowns	224	39		174	198	255	75	
Early morning. 'Come, prepare him'	+118							
Finished the strife	+122							
First of all the week				377				
For this purpose		358			255		110	

	AMR	MP	JP	HTC	CFW	H&P	SOF	other
God of glory, we exalt your name		376			337		136	
God's not dead			60					
Good Joseph had a garden	438					195		
Hallelujah, for the Lord our God		65	66				147	
He is Lord, he is Lord		69	75	s7	586	256	159	
Holy is the Lamb							169	
I am the bread of life		80		s10		611	182	
I know that my redeemer lives		86	169		295	196		
I live, I live, because he is risen		415					202	
I stand before the presence		422					229	
I was once in darkness							248	
In Christ shall all be made alive				459				
In the tomb so cold they laid him		438					4/60	
Jesus Christ is alive today		117	129					
Jesus Christ is risen today	134	447	130	155	242	193	269	
Jesus is Lord		119	137	s17	286	260	278	
Jesus lives! Thy terrors now	140	454		156	262	198		
Jesus, stand among us in your risen		125		364		530	291	
Jesus, we celebrate your victory		707					4/85	
Led like a lamb (You're alive)		282	151		253		307	
Light has dawned		719					4/100	
Light's glittering morning	602			157				
Lord, enthroned in heavenly splendour	400	476		416		616	336	
Lord Jesus Christ, you have come to us	+58	480	156	417	390	617	342	
Lord, the light of your love		714					4/110	
Love's redeeming work is done	141				259			
Low in the grave he lay		150	159	158		202	356	
My Lord, what love is this		***					90/91	
Now lives the Lamb of God				159	246			
O Lord, you are my light		513					412	
Rejoice, the Lord is King	216	195		180	301	243	463	
Rejoice! The Lord is risen		545						
Saviour of the world, thank you		550						
Sing alleluia to the Lord		204		s22	565		476	
Thank you, Jesus		216	235				500	
The day of resurrection	132			161		208		
The Lord is risen indeed	142							

	AMR	MP	JP	HTC	CFW	H&P	SOF	other
Thine be the glory	+95	238	299	167	263	212	545	
This is the day, this is the day		239	255	s28	319	578	547	
This joyful Eastertide			256	165		213		
Victory		252					562	
What a wonderful saviour is Jesus			274		567			
When Easter to the dark world came						200		
You choirs of new Jerusalem	128			168		823		
You laid aside your majesty		644					638	

Easter 1: (1) the Upper Room
(2) the Bread of Life

	AMR	MP	JP	HTC	CFW	H&P	SOF	other
All creatures of our God and King	172	287		13	283	329		
Alleluia, alleluia, give thanks		9	3	s3	252	250	5	
Alleluia! Sing to Jesus	399	67		170		592	151	
Almighty God, we thank you							4/5	
As the disciples, when thy Son	+8							
Bread of heaven, on you we feed	411			398				
Bread of the world, in mercy broken	409			396		599		
Break now the bread of life		316			614	467	46	
Broken for me		318		s6	40			
Christ is the heavenly food	+106							
Christ the Lord is risen again	136	324		153	258	192		
Come on and celebrate		330					69	
Come sing the praise of Jesus		332		208	250			
Come ye faithful, raise the anthem	222	***		205		813		
Dear Lord and Father of mankind	184	40	37	356		673	76	
Fellowship sweet							102	
Glorious things of thee are spoken	257	59		494	183	817	123	
Great shepherd of your people	247			363		490		
Guide me, O thou great Jehovah	286	63		528	129	437	144	
He is Lord, he is Lord		69	75	s7	586	256	159	
His banner over me is love			73					
I am the bread		686						
I am the bread of life		80		s10		611	182	
I hunger and I thirst	413			409		730		
I know that my redeemer lives		86		169	295	196		
I'm feeding on the living bread			104					

	AMR	MP	JP	HTC	CFW	H&P	SOF	other
Jesus lives! Thy terrors now	140	454		156	262	198		
Jesus, stand among us at the meeting		124					290	
Jesus, stand among us in your risen		125		364		530	291	
Jesus the Lord said: 'I am the bread'		458				137		
Jesus, we thus obey	+144					614		
Led like a lamb (You're alive)		282	151		253		307	
Let us break bread together	+147	470				615		
Lord, enthroned in heavenly splendour	400	476		416		616	336	
Loving shepherd of your sheep	444			305	147			
O holy Father, God most dear	+77							
O Lord, we long to see your face	+79							
Peace to you		730					4/138	
Shout for joy, loud and long				348	260			
Sing to God new songs of worship		560		352	249			
Take, eat, this is my body		570					493	
The first day of the week	+91					576		
The strife is past	135	584		163	243	214		
The trumpets sound		***					90/91	
Thine be the glory	+95	238	299	167	263	212	545	
This is his body							546	
This is the day the Lord has made	43			379	201	577		
Through all the changing scenes	290	246		46	576	73		
We break this bread		750					4/174	
When Easter to the dark world came						200		

Easter 2: (1) the Emmaus Road
(2) the Good Shepherd

	AMR	MP	JP	HTC	CFW	H&P	SOF	other
All people that on earth do dwell	166	6	4	14	367	1	8	
Alleluia, alleluia, give thanks		9	3	s3	252	250	5	
Be known to us in breaking bread				410		597		
Because he died and is risen					568			
Broken for me		318		s6	40			
Christ the Lord is risen again	136	324		153	258	192		
Christ who knows all his sheep	+14							
Come, let us, who in Christ believe						755		
Come, risen Lord	+16			399		605		
Enthrone thy God within thy heart						692		

	AMR	MP	JP	HTC	CFW	H&P	SOF	other
Faithful shepherd, feed me	415			29	571			
Father of peace, and God of love						218		
Follow me, says Jesus			46					
For the bread which you have broken	+123			403	46			
For this purpose		358			255		110	
God is good – we sing and shout it		370	55		377		131	
Great shepherd of your people	247			363		490		
Hallelujah, for the Lord our God		65	66				147	
He is Lord, he is Lord		69	75	s7	586	256	159	
He is our peace							160	
I come with joy to meet my Lord	+140			408	16	610		
I receive your love		418					226	
I will sing the wondrous story		101	127	212		223	266	
In Adam we have all been one	+141					420		
It is a thing most wonderful	435	110	117	131	232	224		
Jerusalem the golden	278			573				
Jesus our Lord, our King and our God	+49							
Jesus the good shepherd is						263		
Jesus, thy wandering sheep behold						772		
Jesus where'er thy people meet	245			371		549		
Led like a lamb (You're alive)		282	151		253		307	
Lord Jesus Christ, you have come to us	+58	480	156	417	390	617	342	
Love divine	205	149		217	387	267	353	
Loving shepherd of your sheep	444			305	147			
Morning has broken		***	166	265	279	635		
Now lives the Lamb of God				159	246			
O how good is the Lord		527	180		376			
O Lord, our guardian and our guide	300			374	124			
O thou who this mysterious bread						621		
O what a gift!		176			33	270		
Praise him, praise him, everybody			201	s21	379	565		
Rejoice, the Lord is King	216	195		180	301	243	463	
See the feast our God prepares					17			
Take this bread I give to you					39			
The God of love my shepherd is	178					43		
The head that once was crowned	218	220		182	289	209	508	
The King of love	197	221	241	44	27	69	513	
The Lord my pasture shall prepare	179							

	AMR	MP	JP	HTC	CFW	H&P	SOF	other
The Lord my shepherd rules my life				45	137			
The Lord's my shepherd	+93	227	243	591		70	526	
The steadfast love of the Lord		229	250		373		541	
There are hundreds of sparrows			246		275			
Thine be the glory	+95	238	299	167	263	212	545	
This is the day, this is the day		239	255	s28	319	578	547	
Thou shepherd of Israel						750		
We come as guests invited		613			35			
We have a gospel to proclaim	+98	617		519	433	465		
What a wonderful saviour is Jesus			274		567			
Worthy is the Lamb		280			45		621	
Yours for ever, God of love	330			556				

Easter 3: (1) the Lakeside
(2) the Resurrection and the Life

	AMR	MP	JP	HTC	CFW	H&P	SOF	other
All creatures of our God and King	172	287		13	283	329		
All heaven declares		649					4/2	
Alleluia, alleluia! Hearts to heaven	137			151				
Alleluia! Sing to Jesus	399	67		170		592	151	
At your feet we fall		308			251		28	
Break now the bread of life		316			614	467	46	
By blue Galilee			23					
Christ is risen! Hallelujah		322						
Come, let us with our Lord arise	+116			375		575		
Crown him with many crowns	224	39		174	198	255	75	
For God so loved the world		664						
God is the strength of my life							133	
God of glory, we exalt your name		376			337		136	
Good Christians all, rejoice and sing	603			154		191		
He is Lord, he is Lord		69	75	s7	586	256	159	
How lovely on the mountains		79	84		421		176	
I am the bread of life		80		s10		611	182	
I know that my redeemer lives		86		169	295	196		
I will sing, I will sing		99	126	s15	517			
In the name of Jesus		109	111				218	
In the tomb so cold they laid him		438					4/60	
Jesus Christ is alive today		117	129					

43

	AMR	MP	JP	HTC	CFW	H&P	SOF	other
Jesus lives! Thy terrors now	140	454		156	262	198		
Jesus, my Lord, let me be near you	+143							
Jesus, stand among us in your risen		125		364		530	291	
Led like a lamb (You're alive)		282	151		253		307	
Lord Jesus Christ, you have come to us	+58	480	156	417	390	617	342	
Love divine	205	149		217	387	267	353	
Love's redeeming work is done	141				259			
Low in the grave he lay		150	159	158		202	356	
Morning has broken		***	166	265	279	635		
Now the green blade rises	+168		174			204		
O Lord, you are my light		513					412	
Rejoice, the Lord is King	216	195		180	301	243	463	
Saviour of the world, thank you		550						
Sing glory, glory, alleluia					254			
The day of resurrection	132			161		208		
There in God's garden	+181							
These are the facts		595		162				
Thine be the glory	+95	238	299	167	263	212	545	
We have a gospel to proclaim	+98	617		519	433	465		
What a wonderful saviour is Jesus			274		567			
You are the way	199	605		113		234		
You give us beauty							636	
You laid aside your majesty		644					638	

Easter 4: (1) *the Charge to Peter*
(2) *the Way, the Truth, and the Life*

	AMR	MP	JP	HTC	CFW	H&P	SOF	other
Abba, Father, let me be		1	2		399		1	
And can it be		11		588	389	216	12	
Christ is the King	+12			492				
Come, let us, who in Christ believe						755		
Come, my way, my truth, my life						254		
Creator of the earth and skies	+18			320		419		
Forth in the peace of Christ	+125			542				
God is here! As we his people	+131			560		653		
God is so good			53		396			
How I love you, you are the one		398					174	
How sweet the name of Jesus sounds	192	78		211		257	178	

LECTIONARY WEEKS

	AMR	MP	JP	HTC	CFW	H&P	SOF	other
I am the way, the truth			89					
I am trusting you, Lord Jesus		81	86	433	406		183	
I believe in God the Father				434	404			
I know that my redeemer lives		86		169	295	196		
Jerusalem the golden	278			573				
Jesus calls us, o'er the tumult	533	116		104		141		
Jesus, how lovely you are		118	133				274	
Jesus, I will come with you			138					
Jesus, my Lord, my God, my all	202			476				
Just as I am	349	132	146	440	411	697	304	
King of glory, King of peace	367	462			157	499		
Light's abode, celestial Salem	279							
Lord, all-knowing, you have found me					394			
Lord Jesus Christ, you have come to us	+58	480	156	417	390	617	342	
Lord, you can make our spirits shine				512				
My hope is built on nothing less		162		462				
O Jesus, I have promised	331	172		531		704	400	
O Lord, my love, my strength				485				
Praise the name of Jesus		189			401		449	
Reign in me, sovereign Lord		546			403		4/142	
Rejoice! Rejoice! Christ is in you		543			538		461	
Risen Lord, whose name we cherish				500				
Safe in the shadow of the Lord		549		445	395			
Salvation is found in no-one else					397			
Sing a new song to the Lord		203		349	420	57		
Take up your cross	333			114				
The nations shall see you justified							527	
To God be the glory		248	259	584	412	463	559	
Yesterday, today, forever		277	294					

Easter 5: *Going to the Father*

	AMR	MP	JP	HTC	CFW	H&P	SOF	other
Alleluia, alleluia, give thanks		9	3	s3	252	250	5	
Alleluia, alleluia! Hearts to heaven	137			151				
Almighty Father, who for us	+5					401		
Amazing grace		10	8	28	158	215	10	
Arise, my soul, arise						217	16	
Children of the heavenly King	295			566	556			

45

	AMR	MP	JP	HTC	CFW	H&P	SOF	other
Christ is the world's redeemer						219		
Christ the Lord is risen again	136	324		153	258	192		
Come and see the shining hope		33		191	578			
Come, ye faithful, raise the anthem	222	***		205		813		
Faithful shepherd, feed me	415			29	571			
Faithful vigil ended	+120	660		55	562			
For this purpose		358			255		110	
From heaven you came		361			449		120	
Give to our God immortal praise	+127	363		31		22		
God of glory, we exalt your name		376			337		136	
God of gods, we sound his praises				340	561			
Guide me, O thou great Jehovah	296	63		528	129	437	144	
Hail, our once-rejected Jesus		383		175		222	145	
Have faith in God, my heart	+39			431		675		
He is exalted		677					4/34	
Here from all nations				571	577			
How lovely on the mountains		79	84		421		176	
I was glad when they said					559			
Immortal, invisible	372	103		21	267	9	210	
In the presence of the Lord							219	
Jesus, high in glory					214			
Jesus is Lord of all		450					279	
Jesus, Prince and Saviour		456						
Jesus shall take the highest honour		705					4/83	
Join all the glorious names		461		214		78	301	
Love divine	205	149		217	387	267	353	
Love's redeeming work is done	141				259			
Low in the grave he lay		150	159	158		202	356	
Name of all majesty		499		218	306			
Now is eternal life	+69					203		
Now lives the Lamb of God				159	246			
O worship the Lord in the beauty	77	179		344	92	505	429	
Rejoice, the Lord is King	216	195		180	301	243	463	
Sing alleluia to the Lord		204		s22	565		476	
Soon and very soon		208	221		566			
The King of love	197	221	241	44	27	69	513	
The Lord my shepherd rules my life				45	137			
There is a land of pure delight	285			575		822		
This is the day the Lord has made	43			379	201	577		

	AMR	MP	JP	HTC	CFW	H&P	SOF	other
This is the day, this is the day		239	255	s28	319	578	547	
To God be the glory		248	259	584	412	463	559	
To him who sits on the throne							4/166	
We are chosen, we are redeemed							568	
We are more than conquerors							573	
What a wonderful saviour is Jesus			274		567			
When all your mercies, O my God	177	***		39	383	573		
Worthy is the Lamb		280			45		621	
You, O Lord							4/196	

Ascension: *the Ascension of Christ*

	AMR	MP	JP	HTC	CFW	H&P	SOF	other
All hail the Lamb		648					4/1	
All hail the power of Jesus' name	217	5		587		252	7	
All heaven declares		649					4/2	
Alleluia! Sing to Jesus	399	67		170		592	151	
At the name of Jesus	225	15	13	172	305	74	26	
Christ triumphant, ever reigning		28	25	113	300			
Come, let us join our cheerful songs	221	37		206	555	810	64	
Crown him with many crowns	224	39		174	198	255	75	
Father in heaven how we love you		661					4/22	
Father in heaven, our voices we raise		662					4/21	
Father, we adore you, you've drawn us		352					97	
For his name is exalted		357					108	
For thou O Lord art high		53					112	
For we see Jesus							114	
Give to our God immortal praise	+127	363		31		22		
Glory, glory in the highest		668					4/29	
Glory in the highest				582	25			
God forgave my sins (Freely, freely)		60	54	s12	293		126	
God has exalted him					294		129	
Hail the day that sees him rise	147	382		176		197		
Holy, holy, holy is the Lord		74			338		166	
Immortal, invisible	372	103		21	267	9	210	
In the tomb so cold they laid him		438					4/60	
Jesus is Lord		119	137	s17	286	260	278	
Jesus, name above all names		122	141		226		288	
Jesus, our hope, our heart's desire	146			178				

	AMR	MP	JP	HTC	CFW	H&P	SOF	other
Jesus shall reign where'er the sun	220	123		516	415	239	289	
Jesus, you are the radiance		460					298	
Lift high the cross	633	139		508		170		
Look, you saints, the sight		475		179		201	334	
Majesty – worship his majesty		151	160		339		358	
Name of all majesty		499		218	306			
O come let us worship		505					390	
O Lord our God (We will magnify)		512					409	
Our eyes have seen the glory		535	191					
Our Lord is risen from the dead	609					206		
Praise him, praise him, Jesus		186	203		304		439	
Reigning in all splendour		732					459	
See the conqueror mounts in triumph	148			181				
Sovereign Lord				s9			485	
The Lord ascendeth up on high						210		
There is a redeemer		590			228		534	
There's no greater name		236		s27				
Thy hand, O God, has guided	256	247	298	536	130	784		
To him who sits on the throne							4/166	
Where high the heavenly temple stands	204			184				
Worthy is the Lamb		635					622	
Ye servants of God	226	278		520		278	628	
You laid aside your majesty		644					638	
You, O Lord							4/196	

Pentecost

	AMR	MP	JP	HTC	CFW	H&P	SOF	other
All heaven waits with bated breath		290					4/3	
All over the world the Spirit		293	5					
As we seek your face							90/91	
Breathe on me, breath of God	236	25		226	326	280	47	
Burn, Holy Fire							49	
Colours of day (Light up the fire)			28					
Come down, O love divine	235	34		231	308	281		
Come, gracious Spirit	232							
Come Holy Ghost, our souls inspire	157	36		589		283		
Come, Holy Spirit, come							4/14	

	AMR	MP	JP	HTC	CFW	H&P	SOF	other
Come, most Holy Spirit, come	156			227	327	284		
Falling, falling, gently falling					315			
Father, we adore you		44	44	s5	191		96	
Father, we adore you, you've drawn us		352					97	
Father, we love you		46	45		336		98	
Filled with the Spirit's power	+26			233		314		
God whose Son was once a man on earth		380	62					
God's Spirit is in my heart					422	315		
Gracious Spirit, Holy Ghost	233	377		474	476	301		
Hail thee, festival day						302		
Hear, O Lord, our cry							90/91	
Holy Spirit, truth divine				235	322	289		
Holy Spirit, we welcome your presence							4/41	
I can almost see							4/48	
I hear the sound of rustling		88					197	
It's the presence of your Spirit, Lord							236	
Jesus is Lord		119	137	s17	286	260	278	
Jesus, we celebrate your victory		707					4/85	
Like a candle flame		712						
Lord, come and heal your church		716					4/101	
Lord of the church, we pray		485		499				
Lord, the light of your love		714					4/110	
Lord, we long for you		713					4/113	
O breath of life, come sweeping		164		237	464	777	388	
O Holy Spirit, breathe on me		170			316			
O Holy Spirit, come to bless	234			238	475			
O thou who camest from above	329	174		552		745	424	
On the day of Pentecost	+171							
Our blest redeemer, ere he breathed	230	529		241		312		
River, wash over me		548					468	
Spirit divine, inspire our prayers	239	563		240	309	327		
Spirit of God, unseen as the wind					609			
Spirit of the living God, fall		736					4/152	
Spirit of the living God, fall		209	222	s23	317	295		
Spirit of the living God, move				s24	318			
The King is among us		222			6		511	

	AMR	MP	JP	HTC	CFW	H&P	SOF	other
There is a redeemer		590			228		534	
This is the day, this is the day		239	255	s28	319	578	547	
We'll walk the land		***						
Wind, wind blow on me		631						

Pentecost 1: Trinity Sunday

	AMR	MP	JP	HTC	CFW	H&P	SOF	other
All my hope on God is founded	+3	292		451		63		
Angel voices, ever singing	246	304		307		484	15	
Christ is the world's redeemer						219		
Creator Spirit, by whose aid						285		
Father all-loving	+22(ii)							
Father, Lord of all creation	+23							
Father of heaven, whose love profound	164			359		519		
Father, Son, and Holy Ghost						791		
Father, we love you		46	45		336		98	
Father, you're enthroned							4/24	
Glory be to God in heaven				581	24			
Glory be to God in heaven		364						
Go forth and tell		61		505	506	770		
God whose almighty word	266	244		506	416	29		
God whose Son was once a man on earth		380	62					
Hail! Holy, holy, holy, Lord						6		
Holy, holy, holy, holy		75		s14				
Holy, holy, holy is the Lord		74			338		166	
Holy, holy, holy, Lord God Almighty	160	73		7	329	7	168	
Holy is the Lord our God		681					4/40	
How lovely on the mountains		79	84		421		176	
I bind myself to God today	162			5		695		
I want to thank you		694						
Immortal, invisible	372	103		21	267	9	210	
In the presence of your people		108			334		220	
Jesus Christ our great redeemer		706					270	
Jesus, how lovely you are		118	133				274	
Jesus is King, and I will extol		449			169		277	
Jesus, King of kings							4/80	
Let all mortal flesh keep silence	390			61		266		

	AMR	MP	JP	HTC	CFW	H&P	SOF	other
Lifted high, exalted Father God							325	
Lord of the boundless curves of space	+160					335		
Majesty – worship his majesty		151	160		339		358	
O breath of God, breathe on us now						308		
O Father, I do love you							391	
O worship the King	167	178		24	351	28	428	
Precious Father							456	
River, wash over me		548					468	
Sing we praise to God the King					333			
The Lord is King, he is mighty		742			537		520	
Three in one, and one in three	163			12	346			
We believe in God the Father		611						
We give immortal praise	+187			11		18		
Ye watchers and ye holy ones	+199							
You are the King of glory		279	296		211		630	

Pentecost 2: (1) the People of God
(2) the Church's Unity and Fellowship

	AMR	MP	JP	HTC	CFW	H&P	SOF	other
A new commandment		283		s26	445		14	
An army of ordinary people		301					11	
As we are gathered		13					24	
As your family, Lord						595		
Bind us together, Lord		21	17	s4	119		39	
Blest be the dear uniting love						752		
Blest be the tie that binds		311				754		
Brothers and sisters			21					
Children of the heavenly King	295				566	356		
Christ is our corner-stone	243				564	482		
City of God, how broad	258					809		
Come, and let us sweetly join						756		
Come and praise him, royal priesthood		31					58	
Come, let us join our friends above	628					812		
Come, walk with me							72	
Command thy blessing from above						488		
Father, hear the prayer we offer	182	43	41	360	85	436		
Father, I give you the whole of my life							93	

	AMR	MP	JP	HTC	CFW	H&P	SOF	other
Father, make us one		349					95	
Fellowship sweet							102	
For I'm building a people of power		50	47		469		109	
Glorious things of thee are spoken	257	59		494	183	817	123	
God is here! As we his people	+131			560		653		
Gracious Spirit, Holy Ghost	233	377		474	476	301		
Guide me, O thou great Jehovah	296	63		528	129	437	144	
He wants not friends						495		
Head of the church, our risen Lord						547		
Help us to help each other, Lord	+41			540	439			
Hévénu shalóm aléchem		396						
How good a thing it is				497	116			
I am joined to the perfect life							181	
I come to you in Jesus' name							90/91	
I have built in my people							193	
I love you with the love of the Lord							205	
I sing a song of the saints			115					
I will build my church		695					4/67	
If my people, who bear my name		697					4/50	
If there be any love between us							187	
If your heart is right with my heart							188	
In Christ there is no east or west	+43	435		322	429	758		
Jesus, King of kings							4/80	
Jesus, stand among us at the meeting		124					290	
Join our hands with yours							302	
Let all the world in every corner	375	135		342	49	10		
Let saints on earth in concert sing	272	466		574				
Let there be love shared among us		137			58		318	
Let us open up ourselves							323	
Let us praise God together			152	s18	438			
Living under the shadow of his wing		474					331	
Lord, come and heal your church		716					4/101	
Lord of the church, we pray		485		499				
Lord, please make your people one							345	
Make me a channel of your peace		153	161	s19	470	776		
Make us one, Lord							90/91	
May the grace of Christ our saviour	636			370	504	762		
O Holy Spirit, come to bless	234			238	475			

	AMR	MP	JP	HTC	CFW	H&P	SOF	other
O Lord, our guardian and our guide	300			374	124			
O thou who at thy Eucharist	402					779		
One must water, one must weed					471			
Praise God for the body							435	
Pray that Jerusalem may have peace						510		
Revive your church, O Lord	362	198		515	479	780	465	
Stand up, and bless	374	210	224	351		513	487	
Sweet fellowship							492	
The Church of God a kingdom is	254							
The church's one foundation	255	217		501		515	505	
The church's one foundation							4/157	
Through all the changing scenes	290	246		46	576	73		
Thy hand, O God, has guided	256	247	298	536	130	784		
We are a chosen people		607					565	
We are being built into a temple					491		567	
We are in God's army							4/170	
We are one body in the Lord					120			
We are your people							4/172	
We have a gospel to proclaim	+98	617		519	433	465		
We'll walk the land		***						
Where love and loving-kindness dwell	+195							
You are the vine		643					633	
You have been given							4/194	
You've joined our hearts							645	

Pentecost 3: (1) the Life of the Baptised
(2) the Church's Confidence in Christ

	AMR	MP	JP	HTC	CFW	H&P	SOF	other
All my hope on God is founded	+3	292		451		63		
All the way, all the way		296			207			
Amazing grace		10	8	28	158	215	10	
Ascribe greatness		14					18	
At the name of Jesus	225	15	13	172	305	74	26	
Be thou my vision	+10	17		545		378	38	
Bind us together, Lord		21	17	s4	119		39	
Breathe on me, breath of God	236	25		226	326	280	47	
Christ in me is to live					140			
Christ is our corner-stone	243			564	482			

	AMR	MP	JP	HTC	CFW	H&P	SOF	other
Christ, when for us you were baptised	+109					129		
Christians, lift up your hearts	+113			383				
Cleanse me from my sin, Lord		30	27		225			
Come down, O love divine	235	34		231	308	281		
Faithful shepherd, feed me	415			29	571			
Father, I place into your hands		45	42				94	
For I'm building a people of power		50	47		469		109	
For this purpose		358			255		110	
Gracious Spirit, Holy Ghost	233	377		474	476	301		
Have thine own way, Lord		386					153	
Have you heard the raindrops			71					
He has shown you, O man		675					4/33	
Help us to help each other, Lord	+41			540	439			
How sweet the name of Jesus sounds	192	78		211		257	178	
I am persuaded (More than conquerors)							4/45	
I come to you in Jesus' name							90/91	
I get so excited, Lord, ev'ry time		410					189	
I have decided to follow Jesus		84	98					
I love you, my Lord							204	
If you want joy			96					
I'm saved by the grace of God							212	
In Christ there is no east or west	+43	435		322	429	758		
It's your blood		701					4/62	
Jesus bids us shine			128					
Jesus is Lord		119	137	s17	286	260	278	
Jesus, Jesus loves . . . yes he does					7			
Jesus the very thought of thee	189	129		478		265	295	
Jesus, you are changing me		459					297	
Jesus, you are the power		709					4/86	
Keeping my eyes upon you, Lord							4/90	
Let all the world in every corner	375	135		342	49	10		
Lift high the cross	633	139		508		170		
Lord Jesus Christ, you have come to us	+58	480	157	417	390	617	342	
Lord of the church, we pray		485		499				
Lord, we give you praise							4/112	
Make me a channel of your peace		153	161	s19	470	776		
May the mind of Christ		157	165	550	452	739		

	AMR	MP	JP	HTC	CFW	H&P	SOF	other
My God, accept my heart this day	459			551		701		
My heart is full of Christ						799		
Now is eternal life	+69					203		
O for a thousand tongues	196	168		219		744	394	
O Holy Spirit, come to bless	234			238	475			
O Jesus, I have promised	331	172		531		704	400	
O Lord, you're beautiful		514					413	
Rejoice in the Lord always		194	208				462	
Soldiers of Christ, arise	303	207		533	529	719	483	
Spirit of the living God, move				s24	318			
Take my life, and let it be	361	212		554	151	705	496	
Thank you for ev'ry new good morning			230					
The church's one foundation							4/157	
The King of love	197	221	241	44	27	69	513	
The Lord my shepherd rules my life				45	137			
This day God gives me	+183							
To the name of our salvation	190			222		80		
We are being built into a temple					491		567	
We are one body in the Lord					120			
We'll walk the land		***						
When Jesus came to Jordan	+193					132		
Ye servants of God	226	278		520		278	628	
Your mercy flows							4/199	

Pentecost 4: (1) the Freedom of the Sons of God
(2) the Church's Mission to the Individual

	AMR	MP	JP	HTC	CFW	H&P	SOF	other
Abba, Father, let me be		1	2		399		1	
All ye who seek for sure relief	104							
And can it be		11		588	389	216	12	
Ask! Ask! Ask!			11					
Behold the amazing gift of love						666		
Behold what manner of love			15					
Christ who knows all his sheep	+14							
Come, O thou traveller unknown	343					434		
Father, who in Jesus found us	+25					607		
For God so loved the world					402			

	AMR	MP	JP	HTC	CFW	H&P	SOF	other
God is so good			53		396			
Have faith in God, my heart	+39			431		521		
How shall they hear, who have not		402		507				
I am a new creation		404			359		179	
I heard the voice of Jesus say	351	85				136	196	
I will sing the wondrous story		101	127	212		223	266	
Jesus, Lord, we look to thee	+47					759		
King of glory, King of peace	367	462			157	499		
Lord, all-knowing, you have found me					394			
Lord Jesus Christ, you have come to us	+58	480	156	417	390	617	342	
Lord make me a mountain		483						
Lord of all hopefulness	+61		157	101	86	552		
Love one another							355	
Make me a captive, Lord		152				714		
O breath of life, come sweeping		164		237	464	777	388	
O for a heart to praise my God	325	167		483		536	393	
O thou not made with hands	259					656		
One shall tell another		531			30		417	
Peace is flowing like a river		183					431	
Praise the name of Jesus		189			401		449	
Reign in me, sovereign Lord		546			403		4/142	
Remember all the people			207					
Salvation is found in no-one else					397			
Show your power, O Lord		734					4/148	
The God who rules this earth	+92							
There is a green hill far away	214	230	245	148	219	178	532	
There's a new wave coming							4/163	
To God be the glory		248	259	584	412	463	559	
We are his children (Go forth)							90/91	
We are marching in the great		609						
We've a story to tell		261	272					
When to our world the Saviour came		627						
Ye that know the Lord is gracious	260							
Your mercy flows							4/199	
Yours for ever, God of love	330			556				

Pentecost 5: (1) the New Law
(2) the Church's Mission to All Mankind

	AMR	MP	JP	HTC	CFW	H&P	SOF	other
All things are possible to them						723		
Awake, awake, fling off the night	+9							
Blest are the pure in heart	335	313		110		724	40	
Christ, when for us you were baptised	+109					129		
Father all-loving	+22(ii)							
Forth in the peace of Christ	+125			542				
From all that dwell below the skies	630			580	419	489	118	
From the sun's rising		666					4/26	
Go forth and tell		61		505	506	770		
Go, tell it on the mountain			65		424	135		
God forgave my sins (Freely, freely)		60	54	s12	293		126	
God is working his purpose out	271	373	57	188		769	134	
God whose almighty word	266	244		506	416	29	554	
He's got the whole (wide) world		390	78		189	25		
Head of thy church, whose Spirit fills						316		
How lovely on the mountains		79	84		421		176	
If you see someone			95					
In Christ there is no east or west	+43	435		322	429	758		
Jesus put this song into our hearts		457			423		4/81	
Let all the world in every corner	375	135		342	49	10		
Lord, as I wake I turn to you	+152			267	162	634		
Lord make me a mountain		483						
Lord, thy church on earth is seeking				511		774		
Of all the Spirit's gifts to me	+170					320		
Raise up an army							4/141	
Said Judas to Mary			211					
Send me out from here, Lord		556			425			
Shout it in the street						782		
Tell all the world of Jesus				521	434			
The day you gave us, Lord, is ended	33	218	236	280	436	648	506	
There's a spirit in the air	+182			245		326		
This is the truth which we proclaim				388	2			
We are his children (Go forth)							90/91	
We are marching in the great		609						
We have a gospel to proclaim	+98	617		519	433	465		
We've a story to tell		261	272					

	AMR	MP	JP	HTC	CFW	H&P	SOF	other
We've been called to change the world							4/179	
When Christ was lifted from the earth	+192			335				
With joy we meditate the grace	+197	***				235		
You are the way	199	605		113		234		

Pentecost 6: *the New Man*

	AMR	MP	JP	HTC	CFW	H&P	SOF	other
Awake, awake, fling off the night	+9							
Bind us together, Lord		21	17	s4	119		39	
Breathe on me, breath of God	236	25		226	326	280	47	
Christian people, raise your song	+110					601		
Come down, O love divine	235	34		231	308	281		
Come, let us with our Lord arise	+116			375		575		
Eternal ruler of the ceaseless round	+20							
For I'm building a people of power		50	47		469		109	
Give me joy in my heart	+126			s11	446	492		
Give me oil in my lamp		58	50					
Gracious Spirit, Holy Ghost	233	377		474	476	301		
He has shown you, O man		675					4/33	
I am a new creation		404			359		179	
I have decided to follow Jesus		84	98					
I heard the voice of Jesus say	351	85				136	196	
I will change your name							4/68	
I will sing the wondrous story		101	127	212		223	266	
If there be any love							187	
Immortal love, for ever full	208	***		105		392		
Jesus, Lord, we look to thee	+47					759		
Just as I am	349	132	146	440	411	697	304	
Let me have my way among you		134					312	
Lord God, by whom all change						39		
Lord God, your love has called us	+156			480		500		
Lord, you set my heart on fire							4/117	
Make me a channel of your peace		153	161	s19	470	776		
Now is eternal life	+69					203		
O for a closer walk with God	326	166		368			392	
O Holy Spirit, come to bless	234			238	475			
O Holy Spirit, Lord of grace	231					310		

	AMR	MP	JP	HTC	CFW	H&P	SOF	other
One must water, one must weed					471			
Praise, my soul, the King of heaven	365	187	204	38	459	13	441	
Reign in me, sovereign Lord		546			403		4/142	
Spirit of the living God fall		736					4/152	
There in God's garden	+181							
To God be the glory		248	259	584	412	463	559	
We are being built into a temple					491		567	
What Adam's disobedience cost	+191					430		
When the Spirit of the Lord					472		604	
You brought me back							4/191	

Pentecost 7: *the More Excellent Way*

	AMR	MP	JP	HTC	CFW	H&P	SOF	other
A new commandment		283		s26	445		14	
And can it be		11		588	389	216	12	
Caring, sharing, loving, giving					488			
Church of God, elect and glorious					504	444		
Come, let us all unite and sing						31		
Do you want to be a pilot			40					
Don't build your house			39					
Forgive our sins as we forgive					111		134	
From heaven you came		361			449		120	
Give me oil in my lamp		58	50					
God of mercy, God of grace	264				293	527		
Gracious Spirit, Holy Ghost	233	377			474	476	301	
He has shown you, O man		675					4/33	
Help us to help each other, Lord	+41				540	439		
I walk with God							239	
I want to live for Jesus every day			122					
I want to serve the purpose of God							4/64	
I want to thank you		694						
In humble gratitude	+44							
Jesus I will come with you			138					
Jesus put this song into our hearts		457			423		4/81	
Jesus, you are changing me		459					297	
Let there be love shared among us		137			58		318	
Let us praise God together			152	s18	438			
Love divine	205	149			217	387	267	353

	AMR	MP	JP	HTC	CFW	H&P	SOF	other
Make me a channel of your peace		153	161	s19	470	776		
May my life (Sacrificial love)							90/91	
May the mind of Christ		157	165	550	452	739		
O for a heart to praise my God	325	167		483		536	393	
O Jesus, united by thy grace						773		
O thou who camest from above	329	174		552		745	424	
Praise to the Lord, the Almighty	382	192		40	89	16	452	
Reign in me, sovereign Lord		546			403		4/142	
The earth was dark until you spoke		288			447			
We are your people							4/172	
We really want to thank you, Lord		256	268		494		587	
We've been called to change the world							4/179	
What does the Lord require	+99					414		
When I needed a neighbour	+100		275					
Who does Jesus love					144			

Pentecost 8: the Fruit of the Spirit

	AMR	MP	JP	HTC	CFW	H&P	SOF	other
Bind us together, Lord		21	17	s4	119		39	
Christians, lift up your hearts	+113			383				
Come down, O love divine	235	34		231	308	281		
Come, most Holy Spirit, come	156			227	327	284		
Falling, falling, gently falling					315			
Father, we adore you		44	44	s5	191		96	
Father, we love you		46	45		336		98	
Filled with the Spirit's power	+26			233		314		
Give me joy in my heart	+126			s11	446	492		
Give me oil in my lamp		58	50					
God's Spirit is in my heart					422			
Gracious Spirit, Holy Ghost	233	377		474	476	301		
Holy Spirit, come, confirm us	+138					288		
Holy Spirit, truth divine				235	322	289		
I have a destiny							4/52	
Jesus, the gift divine I know						318		
Love divine	205	149		217	387	267	353	
Love, joy, peace and patience			158					
Make me a channel of your peace		153	161	s19	470	776		

	AMR	MP	JP	HTC	CFW	H&P	SOF	other
O breath of life, come sweeping		164		237	464	777	388	
O Holy Spirit, come to bless	234			238	475			
O King enthroned on high	237					311		
Of all the Spirit's gifts to me	+170					320		
On all the earth thy Spirit shower						321		
On the day of Pentecost	+171							
One must water, one must weed					471			
Praise him on the trumpet		539	200		468		438	
Put on the sword of the Spirit					541			
Spirit divine, inspire our prayers	239	563		240	309	327		
Spirit of God, descend upon my heart						313		
Spirit of God, unseen as the wind					609			
Spirit of the living God, fall		209	222	s23	317	295		
The King is among us		222			6		511	
The Spirit came as promised				244	314			
There is a redeemer		590			228		534	
There's a spirit in the air	+182			245		326		
This is the day, this is the day		239	255	s28	319	578	547	
We have a gospel to proclaim	+98	617		519	433	465		
When Jesus came to Jordan	+193					132		
When the Spirit of the Lord					472		604	

Pentecost 9: *the Whole Armour of God*

	AMR	MP	JP	HTC	CFW	H&P	SOF	other
And the warriors							13	
Be bold, be strong		312	14		542		4/9	
Be thou my vision	+10	17		545		378	38	
Christian soldiers, onward go				524	530			
Eternal ruler of the ceaseless round	+20							
Fight the good fight	304	49		526	546	710	103	
For all the saints	527	51		567	550	814		
For this purpose		358			255		110	
God of grace and God of glory	+34	378		324		712		
He that is in us is greater		388					4/37	
I am a wounded soldier		687					4/44	
I hear the sound of rustling		88					197	
I hear the sound of the army		413	100				198	
I may never march in the infantry			101					

	AMR	MP	JP	HTC	CFW	H&P	SOF	other
I will build my church		695					4/67	
In heavenly armour we'll enter		579					4/58	
Jesus, my strength, my hope						680		
Let God arise		467			534		309	
Lord of all hopefulness	+61		157	101	86	552		
March on, my soul, with strength						716		
Not by might but by my Spirit							381	
Oft in danger, oft in woe	291	524		524	530	715		
Onward, Christian soldiers	629	***		532	551	718	419	
Our God is a God of war							426	
Put on the sword of the Spirit					541			
Put thou thy trust in God	310							
Rejoice! Rejoice! Christ is in you		543			538		461	
So we're marching along					543			
Soldiers of Christ, arise	303	207		533	529	719	483	
Soldiers who are Christ's below	524							
Stand up, stand up for Jesus	307	211	226	535		721	489	
Strong in Christ					547			
Thanks be to God who gives us		577			539			
The Lord is King, he is mighty		742			537		520	
The Lord is marching out							4/160	
Through all the changing scenes	290	246		46	576	73		
Through our God we shall do valiantly		600			540		555	
We are in God's army							4/170	
Who is on the Lord's side		274				722	610	
Who would true valour see	293	489	80	590		688		

Pentecost 10: the Mind of Christ

	AMR	MP	JP	HTC	CFW	H&P	SOF	other
A new commandment		283		s26	445		14	
And can it be		11		588	389	216	12	
Blest are the pure in heart	335	313		110		724	40	
Caring, sharing, loving, giving					448			
Church of God, elect and glorious				504	444			
Come, most Holy Spirit, come	156			227	327	284		
Draw me closer, Lord							4/18	
Enthrone thy God within thy heart						692		

	AMR	MP	JP	HTC	CFW	H&P	SOF	other
Ere God has built the mountains						32		
Forgive our sins as we forgive	+29			111		134		
From heaven you came		361			449		120	
Give me oil in my lamp		58	50					
God has exalted him					294		129	
God of mercy, God of grace	264			293	527			
God whose almighty word	266	244		506	416	29	554	
Heavenly Father, may your blessing						473		
Help us to help each other, Lord	+41			540	439			
Holy Spirit, hear us					602	304		
Jesus has sat down		448					273	
Jesus is the name I love							281	
Jesus is the name we worship					166			
Jesus, name above all names		122	141		226		288	
Jesus put this song into our hearts		457			423		4/81	
Let there be love shared among us		137			58		318	
Let us praise God together			152	s18	438			
Lord Christ, who on thy heart	+55					394		
Make me a channel of your peace		153	161	s19	470	776		
May the mind of Christ		157	165	550	452	739		
Now evening comes					461			
O for a heart to praise my God	325	167		483		536	393	
O Jesus my King							401	
O what shall I do					569			
Prepare the way for Jesus to return							457	
Search me, O God			212					
Send me out from here, Lord		556			425			
Son of God, eternal saviour	207			102				
The earth was dark until you spoke		288			447			
There is a redeemer		590			228		534	
We are your people: Lord	+186							
Who does Jesus love					144			

Pentecost 11: the Serving Community

	AMR	MP	JP	HTC	CFW	H&P	SOF	other
A charge to keep I have	328					785		
Alleluia, alleluia, give thanks		9	3	s3	252	250	5	
Almighty Father, who for us	+5					401		

	AMR	MP	JP	HTC	CFW	H&P	SOF	other
Behold the servant of the Lord						788		
Christ is our corner-stone	243			564	482			
Church of God, elect and glorious				504	444			
For the healing of the nations	+28					402		
Forth in the peace of Christ	+125			542				
Forth in thy name	336	55		306		381		
Give me a heart that will love		***						
Give me oil in my lamp		58	50					
Go forth and tell		61		505	506	770		
Go, tell it on the mountain		672	65		424	135		
God forgave my sins (Freely, freely)		60	54	s12	293			
God is love: let heaven adore him	+32	371			368	36		
God's not dead			60					
God's Spirit is in my heart					422	315		
Healing God, Almighty Father		391						
Help us to help each other, Lord	+41			540	439			
How lovely on the mountains		79	84		421		176	
I want to serve the purpose of God							4/64	
If there be any love							187	
If you see someone		95						
Isaiah heard the voice of the Lord		114						
Jesus put this song into our hearts		457			423		4/81	
Jubilate, everybody		130	145				303	
Lord, as we rise	+52							
Lord, give me also							337	
Lord make me a mountain		483						
Lord of the church, we pray		485		499				
Lord, thy church on earth is seeking				511		774		
Make me a channel of your peace		153	161	s19	470	776		
Make me a servant			162					
May my life (Sacrificial love)							90/91	
May the mind of Christ		157	165	550	452	739		
O give thanks to the Lord		182			493		395	
O Lord of heaven and earth and sea	480			287	498	337		
Rejoice! Rejoice! Christ is in you		543			538		461	
Send me out from here, Lord		556			425			
Servant of all, to toil for man						383		
Strengthen for service	+88			423		626		
Tell all the world of Jesus				521	434			

	AMR	MP	JP	HTC	CFW	H&P	SOF	other
The greatest thing in all my life		219	239					
The Lord has led forth his people					121		518	
The Lord has need of me			242					
The Son of God proclaim	+94			415		627		
There's new life in Jesus			249					
This is the truth which we proclaim				388	2			
We have a gospel to proclaim	+98	617		519	433	465		
We love the place, O God	242	618		558	497			
We really want to thank you, Lord		256	268		494		587	
We'll walk the land		***						
What a mighty God we serve		749						
When I needed a neighbour	+100		275					
You are the vine		643					633	

Pentecost 12: the Witnessing Community

	AMR	MP	JP	HTC	CFW	H&P	SOF	other
Brothers and sisters			21					
Caring, sharing, loving, giving					448			
Christ for the world, we sing	+11					789		
Christ is the King! O friends rejoice	+12			492				
Christ is the world's true light	+13			323		456		
Church of God, elect and glorious				504	444			
Colours of day (Light up the fire)			28					
Come on, let's get up and go			31					
Facing a task unfinished		346					88	
Father, make us one		349					95	
Forth in the peace of Christ	+125			542				
From heaven you came		361			449		120	
From the sun's rising		666					4/26	
Give thanks to the Lord, call							90/91	
Go forth and tell		61		505	506	770		
God, your glory we have seen						459		
Here I am		393					161	
How shall they hear, who have not		402		507				
I give you now (Go)							4/51	
I will sing of the love of the Lord							265	
In these last days							221	
Jesus bids us shine			128					

	AMR	MP	JP	HTC	CFW	H&P	SOF	other
Jesus, send more labourers							4/82	
Keep me shining Lord			147					
Let there be glory and honour							317	
Let us talents and tongues employ	+148			414	29			
Lift high the cross	633	139		508		170		
Lord, please make your people one							345	
May your love in me shine							366	
Now dawns the Sun of righteousness		722						
O Lord, I will praise you							404	
O thou who at thy Eucharist	402					779		
Raise up an army							4/141	
Remember all the people			207					
Revive your church, O Lord	362	198		515	479	780	465	
Rise up (Go forth)							4/144	
Seek ye first		201	215		168	138	471	
Send me out from here, Lord		556			425			
Shout it in the street						782		
Show your power, O Lord		734					4/148	
Some folks may ask me							484	
The earth was dark until you spoke		288			447			
The nations are waiting							4/162	
There is no time for holding back							538	
We are his children (Go forth)							90/91	
We have a gospel to proclaim	+98	617		519	433	465		
We shall stand		751					4/178	
We'll walk the land		***						
We've a story to tell		261	272					
Ye servants of God	226	278		520		278	628	

Pentecost 13: the Suffering Community

	AMR	MP	JP	HTC	CFW	H&P	SOF	other
A safe stronghold our God is still	183	284		523		661	17	
All ye who seek for sure relief	104							
Bind us together, Lord		21	17	s4	119		39	
Christ is made the sure foundation		27		559	483	485	54	
Church of God, elect and glorious				504	444			
Commit thou all thy griefs						672		
Father, hear the prayer we offer	182	43	41	360	85	436		

	AMR	MP	JP	HTC	CFW	H&P	SOF	other
Fight the good fight	304	49		526	546	710	103	
For I'm building a people of power		50	47		469		109	
From heaven you came		361			449		120	
Give me oil in my lamp		58	50					
God moves in a mysterious way	181	375				65	135	
God of mercy, God of grace	264			293	527			
He that is down need fear no fall	301					676		
He walked where I walk		678					4/38	
Hear my cry, O God		392						
Here is love							4/35	
In Christ there is no east or west	+43	435		322	429	758		
In the cross of Christ I glory		107			231	167		
Kum ba ya, my Lord			149			525		
Lead us, heavenly Father, lead us	311	465		525	111	68	306	
Let us praise God together			152	s18	438			
Make me a channel of your peace		153	161	s19	470	776		
Now thank we all our God	379	163	175	33	199	566	386	
O God of Bethel	299			35		442		
O Lord, our guardian and our guide	300			374	124			
O love that will not let me go	359	171		486		685	415	
Oft in danger, oft in woe	291	524		524	530	715		
Praise, my soul, the King of heaven	365	187	204	38	459	13	441	
Pray for the church						556		
Saviour from sin I wait to prove						747		
The church's one foundation	255	217		501		515	505	
The head that once was crowned	218	220		182	287	209	508	
Thee will I praise						41		
Through all the changing scenes	290	246		46	576	73		
Through the night of doubt	292			466	128	441		
Thy hand, O God, has guided	256	247	298	536	130	784		
We have come into this house		253		s29	117		581	
Who fathoms the eternal thought						432		
You shall go out with joy		281			118		641	

Pentecost 14: the Family

	AMR	MP	JP	HTC	CFW	H&P	SOF	other
Almighty Father, who for us	+5					401		
Come and praise the Lord our King			34	s8	188			

	AMR	MP	JP	HTC	CFW	H&P	SOF	other
Father God, I wonder how I managed		348					92	
Father God in heaven				358	171			
Father, make us one		349					95	
Father, we adore you		44	44	s5	191		96	
For the beauty of the earth	171	356	48	298	182	333		
For the healing of the nations	+28					402		
God is building a house		369						
God is love – his the care				311	368	220		
God of love and truth and beauty	+35					403		
Have you seen the pussycat			72					
He's got the whole (wide) world		390	78		189	25		
Here we are, gather'd together							4/36	
I come with joy to meet my Lord	+140			408	16	610		
I love to think, though I am young					194			
I will sing, I will sing		99	126	s15	517			
If there be any love between us							187	
If your heart is right with my heart							188	
Jesus, good above all other	+45			96	195	732		
Jesus, Lord, we look to thee	+47					759		
Jesus, the gift divine I know						318		
Jesus where'er thy people meet	245			371		549		
Living under the shadow of his wing		474					331	
Lord Jesus Christ, you have come to us	+58	480	156	417	390	617	342	
Lord of all hopefulness	+61		157	101	86	552		
Lord of the home	+161					367		
Love beyond measure							352	
Now thank we all our God	379	163	175	33	199	566	386	
O love, how deep, how broad	187					229		
O the valleys shall ring		526					423	
One shall tell another		531			30		417	
Praise, my soul, the King of heaven	365	187	204	38	459	13	441	
Tell out, my soul	+89	215	229	42	187	86	498	
Thank you for ev'ry new good morning			230					
Turn the hearts of the children					190			
We are never alone							575	
We are one, we are family							576	
Where cross the crowded ways of life						431		
You've joined our hearts							645	

Pentecost 15: *Those in Authority*

	AMR	MP	JP	HTC	CFW	H&P	SOF	other
All people that on earth do dwell	166	6	4	14	367	1	8	
Bless the Lord, our fathers' God					56			
Bring to the Lord a glad new song				336	54			
Eternal ruler of the ceaseless round	+20							
Father all-loving	+22(ii)							
For I'm building a people of power		50	47		469		109	
For the healing of the nations	+28					402		
God is our strength and refuge		372		527	77			
God is the refuge of his saints						53		
God of mercy, God of grace	264			293	527			
God save our gracious Queen	577	374		592	68	(889)		
Happy the home that welcomes you						366		
Here he comes, robed in majesty					57			
I vow to thee, my country	579							
Judge eternal, throned in splendour		***		329	62	409		
Let all the world in every corner	375	135		342	49	10		
Lift up your heads, you mighty gates	+150					240		
Lord, for the years		142		328	88			
Lord of lords and King eternal	+63							
Lord, you give to us						368		
My God, how wonderful you are	169	498		369	341	51	370	
Now thank we all our God	379	163	175	33	199	566	386	
O God in heaven, whose loving plan	+74					369		
O God, our help in ages past	165	503		37	50	358		
O Lord of heaven and earth and sea	480			287	498	337		
Our Father, by whose name	+172					371		
Praise God from whom all blessings		185	199	585	345		436	
Put on the sword of the Spirit					541			
Rejoice, O land, in God your Lord	582			331				
Rise up, O men of God	+85							
The Lord is a great and mighty King		224			59			
The Lord will come, and not be slow	52					245		
Think of a world without any flowers			254		276	572		
Through all the changing scenes	290	246		46	576	73		
Thy hand, O God, has guided	256	247	298	536	130	784		
Thy kingdom come, O God	262			334	67	783		
We turn to you, O God	+189					412		
When this land knew					55			

	AMR	MP	JP	HTC	CFW	H&P	SOF	other
Ye servants of the Lord	229					248		
Ye that know the Lord is gracious	260							

Pentecost 16: *the Neighbour*

	AMR	MP	JP	HTC	CFW	H&P	SOF	other
A new commandment		283		s26	445		14	
Being of beings, God of love						690		
Caring, sharing, loving, giving					448			
Christians, join in celebration					458			
Come, my soul, thy suit prepare	319					546		
Father, we adore you, you've drawn us		352					97	
For the healing of the nations	+28					402		
Give me joy in my heart	+126			s11	446	492		
Give me oil in my lamp		58	50					
God of mercy, God of grace	264				293	527		
Help us to help each other, Lord	+41				540	439		
Here we are, gather'd together							4/36	
I come with joy to meet my Lord	+140			408	16	610		
It is God who holds the nations						404		
Jesus, Lord, we look to thee	+47					759		
Jesus put this song into our hearts		457			423		4/81	
Let there be love shared among us		137			58		318	
Let us praise God together			152	s18	438			
Lord, as we rise	+52							
Lord make me a mountain		483						
Lord, to you we bring	+162							
Make me a channel of your peace		153	161	s19	470	776		
May the mind of Christ		157	165	550	452	739		
Now join we, to praise the creator	+167					348		
Perfect love							432	
Praise, my soul, the King of heaven	365	187	204	38	459	13	441	
Praise to the Lord, the Almighty	382	192		40	89	16	452	
Son of God, eternal Saviour	207			102				
The Lord is King! Lift up your voice	175	226		183	290	58	519	
The right hand of God						408		
Thy love, O God, has all mankind						411		
We find thee, Lord, in others' need	+97							
We give God thanks				318	453			

	AMR	MP	JP	HTC	CFW	H&P	SOF	other
We pray for peace						413		
We shall be as one							589	
What does the Lord require	+99					414		
When I needed a neighbour	+100		275					
Where love and loving-kindness dwell	+195							
Who does Jesus love					144			

Pentecost 17: the Proof of Faith

	AMR	MP	JP	HTC	CFW	H&P	SOF	other
A safe stronghold our God is still	183	284		523		661	17	
As Jacob with travel was weary	+102					444		
Author of faith, eternal word						662		
Author of life divine	394			395		596		
Be thou my vision	+10	17		545		378	38	
Church of God, elect and glorious				504	444			
Every good gift							83	
Every new day that breaks							84	
Firmly I believe and truly	186			429	145			
Give me oil in my lamp		58	50					
God of grace and God of glory	+34	378		324		712		
God of mercy, God of grace	264			293	527			
God, whose almighty word	266	244		506	416	29	554	
Have faith in God, my heart	+39			431		521		
Have you heard the raindrops			71					
How sweet the name of Jesus sounds	192	78		211		257	178	
I believe in Jesus		688					4/47	
I see perfection		693						
It is no longer I that liveth		445					233	
Jesus is the name we worship					166			
Jesus, we celebrate your victory		707					4/85	
Jesus, you are the power		709					4/86	
Let us praise God together			152	s18	438			
May the mind of Christ		157	165	550	452	739		
Mighty God							4/123	
My faith, it is an oaken staff			168			682		
My God shall supply							4/125	
New every morning is the love	4	161	171	270		636		
Now evening comes					461			

	AMR	MP	JP	HTC	CFW	H&P	SOF	other
O Lord, enlarge our scanty thoughts						568		
O Lord of life, thy quickening voice						637		
O Lord, we long to see your face	+79							
Put thou thy trust in God	310							
Sent forth by God's blessing	+177							
Spirit of faith, come down						325		
This day God gives me	+183							
When my love to Christ grows weak						183		
When our confidence is shaken						686		
When we walk with the Lord		269				687	605	
You never change							4/195	

Pentecost 18: the Offering of Life

	AMR	MP	JP	HTC	CFW	H&P	SOF	other
A charge to keep I have	328					785		
Awake, awake to love and work						631		
Christ is our corner-stone	243			564	482			
Church of God, elect and glorious				504	444			
Come, all you thirsty nations							57	
Come on and celebrate		330					69	
Draw near to God and he'll draw near		339					78	
Enter into his great love							90/91	
Father, I need you							4/20	
Father, you have loved me							100	
Give me the faith		362				767		
Go forth and tell		61		505	506	770		
God is here! As we his people	+131			560		653		
God of light and life's creation				561	505			
'Hallelujah', sing to the Lord		674						
Happiness is to know the Lord			70					
Have you seen the pussycat			72					
How you bless our lives							4/43	
I get so excited, Lord, ev'ry time		410					189	
I live, I live, because he is risen		415					202	
I receive your love		418					226	
I stand before the presence		422					229	
I was glad when they said					559			
I will change your name							4/68	

	AMR	MP	JP	HTC	CFW	H&P	SOF	other
I worship you, O Lamb of God							4/75	
I'm accepted		698					4/56	
In my life, Lord, be glorified		105			495		216	
It is good for me							232	
It's your blood		701					4/62	
Jesus I come							275	
Just as I am	349	132	146	440	411	697	304	
Let us be grateful							321	
Let your living water flow							4/98	
Lord, I will celebrate your love							4/107	
May the grace of Christ our saviour	636			370	504	762		
May the mind of Christ		157	165	550	452	739		
My God, accept my heart this day	459			551		701		
O God, what offering shall I give						801		
O happy day		169	178	442		702		
O Jesus, I have promised	331	172		531		704	400	
O Lord, your tenderness		517					4/131	
Oh, the joy of your forgiveness		724					4/127	
Seek ye the Lord, all ye people		202					472	
Such love, pure as the whitest snow		735					4/152	
Take my life, and let it be	361	212		554	151	705	496	
The Lord has led forth his people		741			121		518	
Victim divine, thy grace we claim						629		
We are being built into a temple					491		567	
We are your people: Lord	+186							
We really want to thank you, Lord		256	268		494		587	
What shall I do my God to love						46		
When I survey	108	265	277	147	238	180	602	
When the road is rough and steep			279					
You came to seek and to save							4/192	

Pentecost 19: the Life of Faith

	AMR	MP	JP	HTC	CFW	H&P	SOF	other
Abba, Father, let me be		1	2		399		1	
All my life, Lord, to you		297						
All the way, all the way		296			207			
Amazing grace		10	8	28	158	215	10	
As Jacob with travel was weary	+102					444		

	AMR	MP	JP	HTC	CFW	H&P	SOF	other
Be thou my vision	+10	17		545		378	38	
Begone, unbelief						667		
Blessed is the man					138			
Cause me to come to thy river, O Lord		319					52	
Create in me a clean heart, O God		334					74	
Father, I place into your hands		45	42				94	
Father, you have loved me							100	
Firmly I believe and truly	186				429	145		
From the sun's rising		666					4/26	
Give me the faith		362				767		
Give me the wings of faith to rise	571					815		
God is our guide			56					
God of my salvation, hear						729		
Great is thy faithfulness		62	64	260	523	66	143	
Have faith in God, my heart	+39			431		675		
Have thine own way, Lord		386					153	
Holiness unto the Lord							90/91	
I am a new creation		404			359		179	
I am persuaded (More than conquerors)							4/45	
I am trusting you, Lord Jesus		81	86	433	406		183	
I believe in God the Father				434	404			
I do not know what lies ahead		409	92					
I want to serve the purpose of God							4/64	
I want to walk with Jesus Christ		444	124	s16	141			
If thou but suffer God to guide thee						713		
It's a happy day			118					
It's your blood		701					4/62	
Jesus, the joy of loving hearts	387	128		413		258	296	
Jesus, you are changing me		459					297	
Leader of faithful souls, and guide						819		
Like a mighty river flowing		145		32	407			
Lord, all-knowing, you have found me					394			
Lord, in full and glad surrender							4/106	
Lord, you're faithful and just							4/116	
May our worship be acceptable		720						
My faith, it is an oaken staff			168			682		
My faith looks up to thee		158				683		

	AMR	MP	JP	HTC	CFW	H&P	SOF	other
My faithful shepherd is the Lord					560			
Nothing but the love of Jesus					398			
O for a closer walk with God	326	166		368			392	
O love divine, how sweet thou art	195					175		
Peace I give to you		538	196					
Praise the name of Jesus		189			401		449	
Put thou thy trust in God	310							
Safe in the shadow of the Lord		549		445	395			
Seek ye first		201	215		168	138	471	
Send me out from here, Lord		556			425			
Sent forth by God's blessing	+177							
So I've made up my mind					143			
Stand up, and bless the Lord	374	210	224	351		513	487	
Surely goodness and mercy			223					
Take my life, and let it be	361	212		554	151	705	496	
The journey of life					210			
The Lord has need of me			242					
The Lord my shepherd rules my life				45	137			
There is a green hill far away	214	230	245	148	219	178	532	
Through all the changing scenes	290	246		46	576	73		
To him we come		602		518	152			
What a wonderful saviour is Jesus			274		567			
When all your mercies, O my God	177	***		39	383	573		
When we walk with the Lord		269				687	605	
Who does Jesus love					144			
Will your anchor hold		275	290			689		
With Jesus in the boat			291					
You are my hiding-place		641					629	

Pentecost 20: Endurance

	AMR	MP	JP	HTC	CFW	H&P	SOF	other
A safe stronghold our God is still	183	284		523		661	17	
Awake, our souls; away, our fears	+103					663		
Be bold, be strong		312	14		542		4/9	
Blessed assurance, Jesus is mine		22	20			668	41	
Christian soldiers, onward go				524	530			
Come, let us join our cheerful songs	221	37		206	555	810	64	
Father, hear the prayer we offer	182	43	41	360	85	436		

	AMR	MP	JP	HTC	CFW	H&P	SOF	other
Fight the good fight	304	49		526	546	710	103	
For all the saints	527	51		567	550	814		
For this purpose		358			255		110	
Give me the wings of faith to rise	571					815		
Glorious things of thee are spoken	257	59		494	183	817	123	
Great is our redeeming Lord						438		
Guide me, O thou great Jehovah	296	63		528	129	437	144	
Have faith in God, my heart	+39			431		675		
Head of thy church triumphant						818		
High in the heavens, eternal God						26		
I am persuaded (More than conquerors)								4/45
I'll praise my maker		427		20		439		
Jesus has died that I might live						733		
Lead, kindly light	298	464				67		
Leader of faithful souls, and guide						819		
Let God arise		467			534		309	
Meet and right it is to sing						501		
Now be strong and very courageous			172					
O happy band of pilgrims	289			530				
O thou who camest from above	329	174		552		745	424	
Oft in danger, oft in woe	291	524		524	530	715		
Onward, Christian soldiers	629	***		532	551	718	419	
Praise the Lord, you heavens	368			583	284	15		
Rejoice! Rejoice! Christ is in you		543			538		461	
Sing we the song of those who stand						821		
Show your power, O Lord		734					4/148	
So we're marching along					543			
Strong in Christ					547			
The church's one foundation	255	217		501		515	505	
The Lord has led forth his people					121		518	
The Lord is my rock							521	
Through our God we shall do valiantly		600			540		555	
Who would true valour see	293	389	80	590		688		

Pentecost 21: *the Christian Hope*

	AMR	MP	JP	HTC	CFW	H&P	SOF	other
All my hope on God is founded	+3	292		451		63		
As Jacob with travel was weary	+102					444		
As pants the hart for cooling streams	314					416		
As the deer pants							22	
Because he died and is risen					568			
Begone, unbelief						667		
Behold, I tell you a mystery					563		33	
Big man standing by the blue waterside			16					
By Christ redeemed, in Christ						600		
Come and go with me					564			
Come, let us with our Lord arise	+116			375		575		
Come, O thou traveller unknown	343					434		
Faithful vigil ended	+120	660		55	562			
Finished the strife	+122							
For you are my God							90/91	
Go labour on, spend, and be spent						794		
God is our guide			56					
God sent his Son		18	58					
Hail to the Lord's anointed	219	64		190		125	146	
Have faith in God, my heart	+39			431		675		
He that is in us is greater		388					4/37	
Here from all nations				571	577			
I am trusting you, O God		432					183	
I do not know what lies ahead		409	92					
I greet thee, who my sure redeemer						391		
I know not why God's wondrous grace							200	
I rest in God alone		690						
I serve a risen Saviour		94	113					
I will wait upon the Lord		426						
Led like a lamb (You're alive)		282	151		253		307	
Lift up your heads, ye gates of brass	306			509		227		
Lord God, thou art our maker	+56							
Love divine	205	149		217	387	267	353	
May the mind of Christ		157	165	550	452	739		
My God, I thank thee		***				564		
Now is eternal life	+69					203		

	AMR	MP	JP	HTC	CFW	H&P	SOF	other
O God, our help in ages past	165	503		37	50	358		
One more step			188			746		
Peace I give to you		538	196					
Put thou thy trust in God	310							
Soon and very soon		208	221		566			
The King of love	197	221	241	44	27	69	513	
The trumpets sound		***					90/91	
Through all the changing scenes	290	246		46	576	73		
Through the night of doubt	292			466	128	441		
What a wonderful saviour is Jesus			274		567			
When our confidence is shaken						686		
Will your anchor hold		275	290			689		
Yesterday, today, forever		277	294					
You, O Lord							4/196	

Pentecost 22: *the Two Ways*

	AMR	MP	JP	HTC	CFW	H&P	SOF	other
A new commandment		283		s26	445		14	
All the way my Saviour leads me		296						
Be thou my vision	+10	17		545		378	38	
Behold, the mountain of the Lord					50			
Change my heart, O God		321					53	
Christ, whose glory fills the skies	7	320		266	134	457		
Christians, join in celebration					458			
Church of God, elect and glorious				504	444			
Cleanse me from my sin, Lord		30	27		225			
Come, let us praise the Lord		653						
Come, most Holy Spirit, come	156			227	327	284		
Don't build your house			39					
From heaven you came		361			449		120	
Give me joy in my heart	+126			s11	446	492		
Give me oil in my lamp		58	50					
God is our guide			56					
God of love and truth and beauty	+35					403		
God of mercy, God of grace	264			293	527			
Have thine own way, Lord		386						
He has shown you, O man		675					4/33	
How shall I sing that majesty	+139					8		

	AMR	MP	JP	HTC	CFW	H&P	SOF	other
I met Jesus at the crossroads			102					
I want to serve you, Lord		700						
In my life, Lord, be glorified		105			495		216	
In the stars his handiwork I see			112					
Jesus is knocking, patiently waiting			135					
King of glory, King of peace	367	462			157	499		
Let there be love shared among us		137			58		318	
Lo, God is here! Let us adore	249					531		
Lord, be thy word my rule	327		250					
Lord of all power, I give you my will	+62		547					
Lord, you set my heart on fire							4/117	
May the mind of Christ		157	165	550	452	739		
My God, accept my heart this day	459			551		701		
O give thanks to the Lord		182			493		395	
O Jesus, I have promised	331	172		531		704	400	
O Lord of heaven and earth and sea	480			287	498	337		
O Lord, our guardian and our guide	300			374	124			
Praise God from whom all blessings		185	199	585	345		436	
Praise to the Lord, the Almighty	382	192		40	89	16	452	
Send me out from here, Lord		556			425			
Sing praises to the Lord				354	490			
Stand up, stand up for Jesus	307	211	226	535		721	489	
Take my life, and let it be	361	212		554	151	705	496	
Teach me your way, O Lord							4/155	
The earth was dark until you spoke		288			447			
The wise man built his house			252					
This is the day, this is the day		239	255	s28	319	578	547	
Though the world has forsaken God			257					
We are being built into a temple					491		567	
We love the place, O God	242	618		558	497			
We really want to thank you, Lord		256	268		494		587	
When the road is rough and steep			279					
Where cross the crowded ways of life						431		
Your will, your way							644	

Pentecost 23: Citizens of Heaven

	AMR	MP	JP	HTC	CFW	H&P	SOF	other
Above the voices of the world		285						
All glory to God in the sky						400		

	AMR	MP	JP	HTC	CFW	H&P	SOF	other
All hail, King Jesus		3					6	
Alleluia, alleluia, give thanks		9	3	s3	252	250	5	
And can it be		11		588	389	216	12	
As we seek your face							90/91	
At your feet we fall		308			251		28	
Before your majesty I stand							32	
Bright the vision that delighted	161			578		445		
Children of the heavenly King	295			566	556			
City, O City							55	
Come and praise the living God		327					59	
Come, let us join our cheerful songs	221	37		206	555	810	64	
Come, workers for the Lord	+17					380		
Father in heaven, how we love you		661					4/22	
Father, we adore you, you've drawn us		352					97	
Fill thou my life	373	48		541		792	104	
From glory to glory	417							
From heaven you came		361			449		120	
Glory, honour, all power be to God							90/91	
God of gods, we sound his praises				340	561			
Great is the Lord, and greatly							141	
Guide me, O thou great Jehovah	296	63		528	129	437	144	
He is exalted		677					4/34	
He who dwells		679						
Holy, holy, holy is the Lord							90/91	
Holy, holy, holy, Lord God Almighty	160	73		7	329	7	168	
Holy is the Lamb							169	
How lovely is thy dwelling-place		399						
How lovely is thy dwelling-place		685					175	
How shall I sing that majesty	+139					8		
I gotta home in Gloryland			97					
I stand before the presence		422					229	
It may be at morn, when the day		443						
Jerusalem the golden	278			573				
Jesus, high in glory					214			
Jesus, Jesus Christ in majesty							283	
Jesus loves me			140	303				
Jesus shall take the highest honour							90/91	

	AMR	MP	JP	HTC	CFW	H&P	SOF	other
King of glory, King of peace	367	462			157	499		
Led like a lamb (You're alive)		282	151		253		307	
Light's abode, celestial Salem	279							
Like a mighty river flowing		145		32	407			
Lo, round the throne	525							
Love divine	205	149		217	387	267	353	
My God, accept my heart this day	459			551		701		
Name of all majesty		499		218	306			
Now unto the King							90/91	
O heavenly Jerusalem	569							
O what their joy	281							
O when the saints			195					
One day when heaven was filled		180	187					
Sing alleluia to the Lord		204		s22	565		476	
Surely goodness and mercy			223					
Ten thousand times ten thousand	284			576				
Thank you, Jesus		216	235				500	
The promised land							529	
The trumpets sound		***					90/91	
There is a land of pure delight	285			575		822		
Therefore the redeemed of the Lord		593					531	
There's a sound on the wind		235					540	
Through all the changing scenes	290	246		46	576	73		
'Tis the church triumphant singing							558	
What a wonderful saviour is Jesus			274		567			
When the Lord in glory comes		628	280	201				
Worthy is the Lamb		280			45		621	
Worthy, O worthy		636			296		624	
Ye holy angels bright	371	637		353		20	627	
You are the Holy One							90/91	
You, O Lord							4/196	

Harvest

	AMR	MP	JP	HTC	CFW	H&P	SOF	other
All creatures of our God and King	172	287		13	283	329		
All people that on earth do dwell	166	6	4	14	367	1	8	
All things bright and beautiful	442	298	6	283	266	330		
Angels praise him, heavens praise him					272			
Bless the Lord, creation sings					163			

	AMR	MP	JP	HTC	CFW	H&P	SOF	other
Come, ye thankful people, come	482	333	32	284	526	355		
Fear not, rejoice and be glad		47			516			
Fill your hearts with joy and gladness		353		30	513			
For the beauty of the earth	171	356	48	298	182	333		
For the fruits of his creation	+124	52		286	522	342		
God of mercy, God of grace	264			293	527			
God who made the earth			63					
God, whose farm is all creation	+37		61	282		344		
Great is thy faithfulness		62	64	260	523	66	143	
I have seen the golden sunshine			99					
I will sing, I will sing		99	126	s15	517			
Jesus is Lord		119	137	s17	286	260	278	
Jesus, send more labourers							4/82	
Let us with a gladsome mind	377	471	154	23	280	27	324	
Now join we, to praise the Creator	+167					348		
Now thank we all our God	379	163	175	33	199	566	386	
Now the green blade rises	+168		174			204		
O Lord of heaven and earth and sea	480			287	498	337		
O worship the King	167	178		24	351	28	428	
One must water, one must weed					471			
Our harvest day is over			193					
Praise and thanksgiving	+82					350		
Praise, O praise our God and King	481					359		
Praise to God, immortal praise	485							
Praise ye the Lord!						338	453	
Sing to the Lord a joyful song						17		
Someone's brought a loaf of bread			220					
Stand up, clap hands			225		274			
The earth is yours, O God				290	514			
The sower went forth sowing	486							
Think of a world without any flowers			254		276	572		
To thee, O Lord, our hearts we raise	484			291	510	362		
We plough the fields, and scatter	483	619	267	292	509	352		
Who put the colours in the rainbow			288		518			
Yes, God is good – in earth and sky		640	293			363		

Remembrance

	AMR	MP	JP	HTC	CFW	H&P	SOF	other
A safe stronghold our God is still	183	284		523		661	17	
All people that on earth do dwell	166	6	4	14	367	1	8	
Behold, the mountain of the Lord						50		
Bless the Lord, our fathers' God					56			
Bring to the Lord a glad new song				336	54			
Christ is the world's true light	+13			323		456		
Come sing the praise of Jesus		332		208	250			
Eternal ruler of the ceaseless round	+20							
Father, hear the prayer we offer	182	43	41	360	85	436		
For the healing of the nations	+28					402		
God is our strength and refuge		372		527	77			
God of mercy, God of grace	264			293	527			
Here he comes, robed in majesty					57			
It is God who holds the nations						404		
Judge eternal, throned in splendour		***		329	62	409		
Lord, for the years		142		328	88			
Lord of lords and King eternal	+63							
Make me a channel of your peace		153	161	s19	470	776		
Make us one, Lord							90/91	
Now thank we all our God	379	163	175	33	199	566	386	
O day of God, draw nigh	+72							
O God of earth and altar						426		
O God, our help in ages past	165	503		37	50	358		
O Lord, the clouds are gathering		728					4/130	
Put thou thy trust in God	310							
Rejoice, O people						657		
Rejoice, the Lord is King	216	195		180	301	243	463	
Tell out, my soul	+89	215	229	42	187	86	498	
The King of love	197	221	241	44	27	69	513	
The Lord is King! Lift up your voice	175	226		183	290	58	519	
The Lord's my shepherd	+93	227	243	591		70	526	
The Saviour's precious blood						410		
Thy hand, O God, has guided	256	247	298	536	130	784		
We turn to you, O God	+189					412		
What does the Lord require	+99					414		
When he comes we'll see just a child		625					599	
When this land knew					55			

	AMR	MP	JP	HTC	CFW	H&P	SOF	other
Where high the heavenly temple stands	204			184				
Ye servants of God	226	278		520		278	628	
Your kingdom come, O God	262			335	67			

THE PSALMS

Introduction to the Psalms

The Psalms have been used by God's worshipping community for many centuries as a book with the special ability to speak to us in every situation. In them we find songs of deep sadness and great joy, loneliness and friendship, silence and noise. The Psalms have always inspired people to write their own versions as offerings of praise and worship to God.

This short list draws together many of these songs to be found in the hymn and song books covered by this list. They are listed by Psalm number, although no attempt has been made to show whether they cover complete Psalms or selected verses, and not every Psalm is represented in the list.

For churches needing more settings it is worth considering two excellent books of Psalms produced by Jubilate Hymns.

Psalms For Today

An excellent book containing metrical settings, responsive arrangements, modern chants, new words to familiar tunes, and settings for canticles and liturgical hymns.

Songs From The Psalms

Another excellent book containing more modern settings of the Psalms, in a wide range of musical styles drawn from many traditions and countries (including the Taizé and Iona communities). Guitar chords are included throughout the book.

A combined words edition is available for the two books which should prove a very valuable aid to churches of all traditions. The book is numbered by Psalm to facilitate ease of use.

PSALMS 1–150

	AMR	MP	JP	HTC	CFW	H&P	SOF	other
Psalm 1								
Blessed is the man					138			
Psalm 2								
No weapon formed		500					385	
Psalm 3								
Lord, enthroned in heavenly splendour	400	476		416		616	336	
Thou, O Lord, art a shield							553	
Psalm 5								
Lord, as I wake I turn to you	+152			267	162	634		
When morning gilds the skies	223	266	278	223		276	603	
There is a name I love to hear		232					533	
Psalm 8								
Angel voices, ever singing	246	304		307		484	15	
How great thou art		173	179				407	
O Lord our God (We will magnify)		512					409	
O Lord, our Lord, how excellent							4/129	
With wonder, Lord, we see your works	+198				271	353		
Your loving-kindness		241					640	
Psalm 9								
O for a thousand tongues	196	168		219		744	394	
O Lord, I will praise you							404	
Psalm 13								
How long will you forget me, Lord					222			
Psalm 16								
Break forth into joy, O my soul		23					45	
In thy presence there's fulness of joy							223	
In the presence of the Lord							219	

86

	AMR	MP	JP	HTC	CFW	H&P	SOF	other
Psalm 17								
O Lord, our guardian and our guide	300			374	124			
Psalm 18								
Ascribe greatness		14					18	
Glorious things of thee are spoken	257	59		494	183	817	123	
I love you, O Lord, you alone		691		475	248			
I will call upon the Lord							250	
I will call upon the Lord		96					251	
It is God who trains my hand for battle							231	
Our God is a God of war							426	
Praise the name of Jesus		189			401		449	
The Lord is my rock							521	
Psalm 19								
All heaven declares		649					4/2	
Lord, your ways are true and just							351	
May our worship be acceptable		720						
The heavens declare your glory, Lord	252			254		481		
The law of the Lord is perfect							514	
Psalm 20								
May the Lord answer you							364	
Psalm 22								
Father in heaven, how we love you		661					4/22	
Father, you're enthroned							4/24	
In the presence of your people		108			334		220	
Jesus, we enthrone you		131					343	
Look and see the glory of the King							333	
Yahweh is holy							4/186	
You, O Lord, are holy							4/197	
Psalm 23								
His name is wonderful		72						
I will rejoice, I will rejoice		424					260	
I will sing the wondrous story		101	127	212		223	266	
In heavenly love abiding		106		458		678	213	

	AMR	MP	JP	HTC	CFW	H&P	SOF	other
My faithful shepherd is the Lord					560			
The God of love my shepherd is	178					43		
The King of love	197	221	241	44	27	69	513	
The Lord my pasture shall prepare	179							
The Lord my shepherd rules my life				45	137			
The Lord's my shepherd	+93	227	243	591		70	526	

Psalm 24

	AMR	MP	JP	HTC	CFW	H&P	SOF	other
Fling wide the gates					291			
Lift up your heads, O ye gates							329	
Lift up your heads to the coming King		473			208		328	
Swing wide the gates		733					4/154	
The earth is the Lord's		748			204			
This earth belongs to God					584			
You are the King of glory		279	296		221		630	

Psalm 25

	AMR	MP	JP	HTC	CFW	H&P	SOF	other
Unto thee, O Lord							561	

Psalm 26

	AMR	MP	JP	HTC	CFW	H&P	SOF	other
We love the place, O God	242	618		558	497			

Psalm 27

	AMR	MP	JP	HTC	CFW	H&P	SOF	other
Jesus the very thought of thee	189	129		478		265	295	
O Lord, you are my light		513					412	
O Lord, you're beautiful		514					413	
Unto thee, O Lord							561	
Wait on the Lord							563	

Psalm 28

	AMR	MP	JP	HTC	CFW	H&P	SOF	other
We rest on thee, our shield		621					588	

Psalm 29

	AMR	MP	JP	HTC	CFW	H&P	SOF	other
Ascribe to the Lord, O heavenly beings							19	
We are stilled by your presence							4/171	
When I look into your holiness		626					601	

Psalm 30

	AMR	MP	JP	HTC	CFW	H&P	SOF	other
Jesus put this song into our hearts		457			423		4/81	

	AMR	MP	JP	HTC	CFW	H&P	SOF	other
Praise, my soul, the King of heaven	365	187	204	38	459	13	441	
Sing praises to the Lord							477	

Psalm 31

	AMR	MP	JP	HTC	CFW	H&P	SOF	other
Be still and know		16	22				37	
Guide me, O thou great Jehovah	296	63		528	129	437	144	
I trust in thee, O Lord		95						
O Jesus, I have promised	331	172		531		704	400	

Psalm 32

	AMR	MP	JP	HTC	CFW	H&P	SOF	other
Lead us, heavenly Father, lead us	311	465		525	111	68	306	
You are my hiding-place		641					629	

Psalm 33

	AMR	MP	JP	HTC	CFW	H&P	SOF	other
Sing joyfully to the Lord					558			

Psalm 34

	AMR	MP	JP	HTC	CFW	H&P	SOF	other
I will bless the Lord at all times							249	
I will magnify your name, O Lord							257	
Jesus – the name high over all		126		213		264	294	
O magnify the Lord with me							416	
O magnify the Lord with me							4/132	
O taste and see that the Lord is good					28		422	
Praise to the Lord! Sing Alleluias							451	
Tell his praise in song and story			41					
Through all the changing scenes	290	246		46	576	73		

Psalm 36

	AMR	MP	JP	HTC	CFW	H&P	SOF	other
How precious, O Lord		400					177	
Jesus, the joy of loving hearts	387	128		413		258	296	
Living under the shadow of his wing		474					331	
Your love, O Lord reaches					370			

Psalm 37

	AMR	MP	JP	HTC	CFW	H&P	SOF	other
Delight yourselves in the Lord		338					77	
The steadfast love of the Lord		229	250		373		541	

Psalm 40

	AMR	MP	JP	HTC	CFW	H&P	SOF	other
Happy are those who trust in God					136			

	AMR	MP	JP	HTC	CFW	H&P	SOF	other
I waited patiently for the Lord					392		238	
O Lord, have mercy on me		510					4/128	
You are the rock on which I stand							4/190	

Psalm 41

	AMR	MP	JP	HTC	CFW	H&P	SOF	other
Stand up and bless the Lord your God							488	

Psalm 42

	AMR	MP	JP	HTC	CFW	H&P	SOF	other
As pants the hart for cooling streams	314					416		
As the deer pants after the water							22	
As the deer pants for the water		303					21	
I will run after you							262	
Lord, I want to know more of you							341	
My soul longs for you							4/126	

Psalm 45

	AMR	MP	JP	HTC	CFW	H&P	SOF	other
I hear the sound of rustling		88					197	
Magnificent warrior							357	
My heart overflows		494					371	
Our God is a God of war							426	
The Lord is marching out							4/160	
Thy throne, O God, is for ever							557	

Psalm 46

	AMR	MP	JP	HTC	CFW	H&P	SOF	other
Be still and know		16	22				46	
Be still, for the presence		652					4/10	
Dear Lord and Father of mankind	184	40	37	356		673	76	
Emmanuel, God is with us							80	
God is our refuge and strength					533			
God is our strength and refuge		372		527	77			
God is the refuge of his saints						53		
Jesus, lover of my soul	193	120		438		528	286	
There is a river							535	

Psalm 47

	AMR	MP	JP	HTC	CFW	H&P	SOF	other
Clap your hands, all you nations					332		56	
God has ascended amid our shouts							127	
Praise to the Lord, the Almighty	382	192		40	89	16	452	
Rejoice, the Lord is King	216	195		180	301	243	463	

	AMR	MP	JP	HTC	CFW	H&P	SOF	other
Sing praises unto God							478	
Take heart and praise our God		740			78			
We dwell in the courts							579	
We will sing praises to the Lord							593	

Psalm 48

	AMR	MP	JP	HTC	CFW	H&P	SOF	other
Great is our redeeming Lord						438		
Great is the Lord, and greatly							141	
Great is the Lord, and most worthy		671						
Great is the Lord, his praise					448			
Guide me, O thou great Jehovah	296	63		528	129	437	144	
How great is God Almighty					313			
I can almost see your holiness							4/48	
Now thank we all our God	379	163	175	33	199	566	386	

Psalm 50

	AMR	MP	JP	HTC	CFW	H&P	SOF	other
Lift up your hands and worship							327	

Psalm 51

	AMR	MP	JP	HTC	CFW	H&P	SOF	other
All the riches of his grace		8						
Change my heart, O God		321					53	
Cleanse me from my sin, Lord		30	27		225			
Cleanse me, O God							4/12	
Create in me a clean heart, O God		334					74	
Have thine own way, Lord		386					153	
It's your blood		701					4/62	
Jesus, come to me							272	
Precious Father, how I love you							456	

Psalm 55

	AMR	MP	JP	HTC	CFW	H&P	SOF	other
Jesus, the joy of loving hearts	387	128		413		413	296	

Psalm 57

	AMR	MP	JP	HTC	CFW	H&P	SOF	other
I will give thanks to thee		98					254	
Living under the shadow of his wing		474					331	

Psalm 59

	AMR	MP	JP	HTC	CFW	H&P	SOF	other
I will sing about your love		425			81		263	

	AMR	MP	JP	HTC	CFW	H&P	SOF	other
Psalm 60								
Through our God we shall do valiantly		600			540		555	
Psalm 61								
Hear my cry, O Lord							154	
Hear my cry, O Lord							155	
Listen to my prayer, Lord				365				
Psalm 62								
I'm expecting great things of you							206	
I rest in God alone		690						
Psalm 63								
Because your love is better than life		19			79		30	
I want to worship the Lord		93					247	
Thy loving-kindness		241					556	
Psalm 65								
O God, it is right for us to praise					512			
The earth is yours, O God				290	514			
Psalm 66								
In him we live and move		433					215	
Let all the world in every corner	375	135		342	49	10		
Psalm 67								
God of mercy, God of grace	264			293	527			
May God be gracious to us				330	270			
Psalm 68								
God is the strength of my life							133	
Let God arise upon this holy mountain							308	
Let God arise, and let his enemies		467			534		309	
Let God arise, let his enemies							310	
Summon your power, O God							491	
We've been called to change							4/179	

	AMR	MP	JP	HTC	CFW	H&P	SOF	other
Psalm 71								
Forth in thy name, O Lord, I go	336	55		306		381		
I will praise you with the harp							90/91	
Psalm 72								
Hail to the Lord's anointed	219	64		190		125	146	
Jesus shall reign where'er the sun	220	123		516	415	239	289	
Prepare the way for Jesus to return							457	
Psalm 73								
It is good for me to draw near to God							232	
Psalm 78								
Guide me, O thou great Jehovah	296	63		528	129	437	144	
Psalm 80								
God is the strength of my life							133	
Hear us, O shepherd of Israel					161			
Psalm 81								
With honey from the rock							615	
Psalm 84								
How lovely is thy dwelling-place		399						
How lovely is thy dwelling-place		685					175	
Lord of the worlds above	248							
My heart's desire is to worship							372	
Pleasant are thy courts above	240							
Psalm 85								
O breath of life, come sweeping		164		237	464	777	388	
Revive your church, O Lord	362	198		515	479	780	465	
When this land knew					55			
Psalm 86								
Come, let us glorify the Lord							63	
I need thee every hour		92				524		
I will give you thanks							256	
I will praise thee, O Lord my God							258	
Teach me your way, O Lord							4/155	

	AMR	MP	JP	HTC	CFW	H&P	SOF	other
Psalm 87								
City, O City							55	
Glorious things of thee are spoken	257	59		494	183	817	123	
I love you, Lord		87					203	
Psalm 89								
Come, join to praise our God					354			
Great is thy faithfulness		62	64	260	523	66	143	
Happy are the people							152	
I have made a covenant							195	
I will sing of the love of the Lord							265	
O I will sing unto you with joy							399	
Timeless love! We sing the story		250		47	372	60		
Psalm 90								
O God, our help in ages past	165	503		37	50	358		
Psalm 91								
Living under the shadow of his wing		474					331	
O Jesus, I have promised	331	172		531		704	400	
Praise to the Lord, the Almighty	382	192		40	89	16	452	
Safe in the shadow of the Lord		549		445	395			
We dwell in the courts							579	
We will sing praises to the Lord							593	
Psalm 92								
I will enter his gates		97					252	
It is a good thing to give thanks							230	
Sweet is the work, my God, my King		568		377		514		
Psalm 93								
Before your majesty I stand							32	
Clothed in kingly majesty				355				
Hallelujah, my Father		66					149	
Magnificent warrior							357	
O Lord our God (We will magnify)		512					409	
Sing we praise to God the King					333			
The Lord reigns, the Lord reigns		584					523	

	AMR	MP	JP	HTC	CFW	H&P	SOF	other
Psalm 95								
Come, let us kneel before him							65	
Come, let us praise the Lord		653						
Come, let us sing for joy to the Lord							4/16	
Come, let us sing to the Lord					393			
Come on, let us sing to the Lord							70	
Come, sing praises to the Lord above					115			
Come with all joy to sing to God				16	205			
Come, worship God who is worthy				18	606			
Let us sing to the God of salvation					186			
Lift up your hands and worship							327	
O come let us sing out to the Lord					786			
O come, let us sing to the Lord					76			
O come, let us worship and bow down		505					390	
O happy day		169	178	442		702		
Psalm 96								
King of kings, Lord of lords							4/92	
O worship the Lord in the beauty	77	179		344	92	505	429	
Sing to the Lord a new song					418			
Sing unto the Lord a new song							481	
The Lord is King! Lift up your voice	175	226		183	290	58	519	
The Lord reigns, let the earth rejoice							524	
Psalm 97								
For Thou O Lord art high		53					112	
The Lord is king! Lift up your voice	175	226		183	290	58	519	
The Lord reigns, let the earth rejoice							524	
Yahweh is King							625	
Psalm 98								
Bless the Lord, O my soul		24	19		80		43	
Blow upon the trumpet				186				
Break forth and sing for joy							44	
Joy to the world! The Lord has come		708		197	664	77	4/88	
King of kings, Lord of lords							4/92	
New songs of celebration render	+165			343		491		
Shout for joy to the Lord							475	

	AMR	MP	JP	HTC	CFW	H&P	SOF	other
Sing a new song to the Lord		203		349	420	57		
Sing to God new songs of worship		560		352	249			
The Lord reigns, let the earth rejoice							524	

Psalm 99

	AMR	MP	JP	HTC	CFW	H&P	SOF	other
Exalt the Lord our God, exalt the Lord		344					86	
Exalt the Lord our God who reigns							87	
Our eyes have seen the King							425	
Sing to the Lord a new song					583			
The Lord reigns, let the earth rejoice							524	
The Lord reigns, let the nations							525	

Psalm 100

	AMR	MP	JP	HTC	CFW	H&P	SOF	other
All people that on earth do dwell	166	6	4	14	367	1	8	
Before Jehovah's awesome throne	370			15		61		
Break forth and sing for joy							44	
Come, rejoice before your maker				17	96			
Come, sing a new psalm of David							71	
God is good, we sing and shout it		370	55		377		131	
I will enter his gates		97					252	
Jubilate, everybody		130	145				303	
Let there be singing							319	
Make a joyful noise unto the Lord							360	
O be glad in the Lord and rejoice					443			
O praise ye the Lord	376	519		354	490		421	
O shout to the Lord in triumph					787			
Praise the Lord, for the Lord is good							443	
Shout for joy and sing							4/147	
Sing to the Lord with joyful voice						61		
We are gathering together		251					569	

Psalm 102

	AMR	MP	JP	HTC	CFW	H&P	SOF	other
The Lord has built up Zion							516	
We are gathering together		251					569	

Psalm 103

	AMR	MP	JP	HTC	CFW	H&P	SOF	other
Bless the Lord, O my soul		26	19		80		43	
Bless the Lord, O my soul		24						
O bless the Lord, my soul				34				
O Lord our God (We will magnify)		512					409	

	AMR	MP	JP	HTC	CFW	H&P	SOF	other
Praise, my soul, the King of heaven	365	187	204	38	459	13	441	
Praise the Lord, my soul					442			
Praise to the Lord, the Almighty	382	192		40	89	16	452	
Ye holy angels bright	371	637		353		20	627	

Psalm 104

	AMR	MP	JP	HTC	CFW	H&P	SOF	other
I will rise and bless you, Lord							261	
Jesus, the very thought of thee	189	129		478		265	295	
O Lord our God, you are very great					104		406	
O worship the King	167	178		24	351	28	428	

Psalm 105

	AMR	MP	JP	HTC	CFW	H&P	SOF	other
Give thanks to the Lord, praise					114			
The Lord has led forth his people		741			121		518	

Psalm 106

	AMR	MP	JP	HTC	CFW	H&P	SOF	other
Love divine	205	149		217	387	267	353	
Thou art my God, and I will praise thee		240					549	

Psalm 107

	AMR	MP	JP	HTC	CFW	H&P	SOF	other
Give thanks to the Lord for he is		667						
Give thanks to the Lord, for he is					487			
I heard the voice of Jesus say	351	85				136	196	
Lift up your heads, you gates of brass				509		227		
Thou art my God, and I will praise thee		240					549	

Psalm 108

	AMR	MP	JP	HTC	CFW	H&P	SOF	other
Through our God we shall do valiantly		600			540		555	

Psalm 111

	AMR	MP	JP	HTC	CFW	H&P	SOF	other
Praise the Lord: with my whole heart					605			

Psalm 113

	AMR	MP	JP	HTC	CFW	H&P	SOF	other
From all that dwell below the skies	630			580	419	489	118	
From the rising of the sun		54	49		139		121	
From the sun's rising		666					4/26	
Praise the Lord: you servants					4			
The day you gave us, Lord, is ended	33	218	236	280	436	648	506	
Ye servants of God	226	278					278	628	

	AMR	MP	JP	HTC	CFW	H&P	SOF	other
Psalm 115								
Not unto us, O Lord							382	
We rest on thee, our shield		621		446			588	
Psalm 116								
I love the Lord because he heard		90			26			
We bring the sacrifice of praise		612					577	
Psalm 117								
Every nation, praise the Lord					97			
From all that dwell below the skies	630			580	419	489	118	
Praise the Lord, all you nations					371			
Psalm 118								
Give thanks to the Lord for he is		667						
Give thanks to the Lord, for he is					487			
God is the strength of my life							133	
I will enter his gates		97					252	
Marvellous in our eyes							363	
Not by might but by my Spirit							381	
Stand up, and bless the Lord	374	210	224	351		513	487	
The Lord is my strength		225					522	
This is the day the Lord has made	43			379	201	577		
This is the day, this is the day		239	255	s28	319	578	547	
Thou art my God and I will praise thee		240					549	
Psalm 119								
God speaks and all things come to be						23		
I will rise and bless you, Lord							261	
O Jesus, I have promised	331	172		531		704	400	
Open thou mine eyes		205						
The will of God to mark my way					607			
When we walk with the Lord		269				687	605	
You are my hiding-place		641					629	
Psalm 121								
I lift my eyes to the quiet hills		416						
Unto the hills around				48				

	AMR	MP	JP	HTC	CFW	H&P	SOF	other
Psalm 122								
I was glad when they said to me					559			
I was glad when they said to me					53			
Let us go to the house of the Lord							4/96	
Pray that Jerusalem may have peace					510			
Psalm 123								
Unto thee do I lift my eyes							560	
Psalm 124								
If the Lord had not been on our side					95			
Psalm 126								
Praise ye the Lord						338	453	
To God be the glory		248	259	584	412	463	559	
When the Lord brought us back					247			
Psalm 128								
Blessed are those who fear the Lord					185			
Psalm 130								
Out of the deep I call	322							
Psalm 132								
My heart overflows		494					371	
Psalm 133								
Father, make us one		349					95	
How good a thing it is				497	116			
Psalm 134								
Angel voices, ever singing	246	304		307		484	15	
Come, bless the Lord		32			795		61	
Come, praise the Lord, all you					486			
Now thank we all our God	379	163	175	33	199	566	386	
We are gathering together		251					569	

	AMR	MP	JP	HTC	CFW	H&P	SOF	other
Psalm 136								
Give thanks to God, for he is good			75					
Give to our God immortal praise	127	363		31		22		
Let us with a gladsome mind	377	471	154	23	280	27	324	
O give thanks to the Lord, all you		182			493		395	
The Lord is marching out							4/160	
Thou art my God and I will praise thee		240					549	
Psalm 138								
I give thanks, O Lord							190	
Psalm 139								
In all my vast concerns						72		
Lord all-knowing, you have found me					394			
Search me, O God		200						
There is no moment of my life					164	428		
Psalm 141								
In through the veil now we enter							222	
Let our praise to you be as incense		468					313	
Psalm 143								
Cause me to come to thy river		319					52	
Jesus, lover of my soul	193	120		438		528	286	
Lift up your hands and worship							327	
O Lord, I spread my hands out to you					312			
Psalm 144								
O worship the King	167	178		24	351	28	428	
Psalm 145								
How good is the God we adore		77		450	84			
I will extol you, my God							253	
One shall tell another		531			30		417	
We would extol thee	380							
Worthy, the Lord is worthy							4/185	
Ye holy angels bright	371	637		353		20	627	

	AMR	MP	JP	HTC	CFW	H&P	SOF	other
Psalm 146								
I will sing unto the Lord		102					267	
I'll praise my maker		427		20		439		
The Lord has given a land		583					517	
You are the King who reigns							631	
Psalm 147								
Fill your hearts with joy and gladness		353		30	513			
Great is the Lord, and mighty							142	
O let the church rejoice					467			
Praise the Lord, for it is good							444	
Praise ye the Lord						338		
Psalm 148								
For his name is exalted		357					108	
O praise ye the Lord	376	519		354	490		421	
Praise him . . . powers and dominations				25				
Praise the Lord from the heavens					269			
Praise the Lord of heaven	381							
Praise the Lord of heaven						507		
Praise the Lord our God					515			
Praise the Lord, you heavens, adore him	368			583	284	15		
Praise to the Holiest in the height	185	191		140		231	450	
Praise to the Lord! Sing Alleluias							451	
When morning gilds the skies	223	266	278	223		276	603	
Ye holy angels bright	371	637		353		20	627	
Psalm 149								
As we come with praise							25	
Bring to the Lord a glad new song				336	54			
Delight yourselves in the Lord		338					77	
I'm gonna dance and sing							207	
Let the high praise of God							314	
Magnificent warrior							357	
My heart's desire is to worship							372	
Not without a cause							384	
Our God is a God of war							426	
Sing a new song – Alleluia					535			

	AMR	MP	JP	HTC	CFW	H&P	SOF	other
Psalm 150								
Bring to the Lord a glad new song				336	54			
Let us praise his name with dancing							4/97	
O praise ye the Lord	376	519		354	490		421	
Praise him in his sanctuary							437	
Praise him on the trumpet		539			468		438	
Praise the Lord, his glories show				345		14		
Praise the Lord: praise God in his		540			466		446	
Praise the Lord, praise him in his							4/140	
Praise the Lord who reigns						55		
Praise to the Lord, the Almighty	382	192		40	89	16	452	
We are gathering together		251					569	

THEMATIC INDEX

Theme	Section
God the Father	
The Commandments	Pentecost 5
The Creation	9 before Christmas
The Fall	8 before Christmas
The Wisdom of God	Epiphany 5
The Whole Armour of God	Pentecost 9
Jesus	
The Advent Hope	Advent 1
The Annunciation	Advent 4
The Ascension of Christ	Easter 5
	Ascension
The Baptism of Jesus	Epiphany 1
Conflict	Lent 2
The Cross	Palm Sunday
	Lent 2 and 3
	Good Friday
The Friend of Sinners	7 before Easter
Going to the Father	Easter 5
The Good Shepherd	Easter 2
The Healer	8 before Easter
The Incarnation	Christmas 1
The Light of the World	Christmas 2
The Mind of Christ	Pentecost 10
The Nativity	Advent 1 to 4
	Christmas Eve and Day
	Christmas 1 and 2
The New Man	Pentecost 6
Parables	Epiphany 6
The Presentation	Christmas 1
The Resurrection and the Life	Easter 3
Signs of Glory	Epiphany 3
The Teacher	9 before Easter
Temptation	Lent 1

Theme	Section
Transfiguration	Lent 4
The Triumphal Entry	Palm Sunday
The Victory of the Cross	Lent 5
The Way, the Truth, and the Life	Easter 4

The Holy Spirit

The Holy Spirit	Pentecost
The Fruit of the Spirit	Pentecost 8
Gifts of the Spirit	Pentecost
	Pentecost 7 and 8
Peace	Easter 1

The Trinity

The Trinity	Pentecost 1

Scripture

The Word of God in the Old Testament	Advent 2

The Church

Baptism	Pentecost 3
The Church's Confidence in Christ	Pentecost 3
The Church's Mission to the Individual	Pentecost 4
The Church's Mission to All Mankind	Pentecost 5
The Church's Unity and Fellowship	Pentecost 2
Commitment	Pentecost 19
Communion	Easter 1
The Serving Community	Pentecost 11
The Suffering Community	Pentecost 13
The Witnessing Community	Pentecost 12
Discipleship	Epiphany 2
The Election of God's People: Abraham	7 before Christmas
Endurance	Pentecost 20
The Holy Family	Christmas 2
	Pentecost 14
Forgiveness	Pentecost 7
Harvest	Harvest

Theme	Section
The New Temple	Epiphany 4
The People of God	Pentecost 2
The Promise of Redemption: Moses	6 before Christmas
Remembrance	Remembrance
The Remnant of Israel	5 before Christmas
Revival	Pentecost
Spiritual Warfare/The Whole Armour of God	Pentecost 9

The Christian Life

The Life of the Baptised	Pentecost 3
Those in Authority	Pentecost 15
Citizens of Heaven	Pentecost 2
The Life of Faith	Pentecost 19
The Proof of Faith	Pentecost 17
The Freedom of the Sons of God	Pentecost 4
The Christian Hope	Pentecost 21
The Offering of Life	Pentecost 18
The Mind of Christ	Pentecost 10
The New Law	Pentecost 5
The Neighbour	Pentecost 16
Service	Pentecost 10 and 11
Suffering	Lent 3
	Pentecost 13
The More Excellent Way	Pentecost 17
The Two Ways	Pentecost 22
Witness	Pentecost 12

Some Significant Biblical Events and Characters

The Election of God's People: Abraham	7 before Christmas
The Emmaus Road	Easter 2
The First Disciples	Epiphany 2
The Forerunner	Advent 3
The Lakeside	Easter 3
The Promise of Redemption: Moses	6 before Christmas
The Charge to Peter	Easter 4
The Upper Room	Easter 1

INDEX OF ASB READINGS

This set of abbreviations for the books of the Bible is used on the following pages.
The same psalms are used for both Year 1 and Year 2.

Old Testament

Gen	Genesis	Eccles	Ecclesiastes
Exod	Exodus	SS	Song of Solomon
Lev	Leviticus	Isa	Isaiah
Num	Numbers	Jer	Jeremiah
Deut	Deuteronomy	Lam	Lamentations
Josh	Joshua	Ezek	Ezekiel
Judges	Judges	Dan	Daniel
Ruth	Ruth	Hosea	Hosea
1 Sam	1 Samuel	Joel	Joel
2 Sam	2 Samuel	Amos	Amos
1 Kings	1 Kings	Obadiah	Obadiah
2 Kings	2 Kings	Jonah	Jonah
1 Chron	1 Chronicles	Micah	Micah
2 Chron	2 Chronicles	Nahum	Nahum
Ezra	Ezra	Hab	Habakkuk
Neh	Nehemiah	Zeph	Zephaniah
Esther	Esther	Haggai	Haggai
Job	Job	Zech	Zechariah
Ps	Psalms	Mal	Malachi
Prov	Proverbs		

New Testament

Matt	Matthew	Phil	Philippians
Mark	Mark	Col	Colossians
Luke	Luke	1 Thess	1 Thessalonians
John	John	2 Thess	2 Thessalonians
Acts	Acts of the Apostles	1 Tim	1 Timothy
Rom	Romans	2 Tim	2 Timothy
1 Cor	1 Corinthians	Titus	Titus
2 Cor	2 Corinthians	Philemon	Philemon
Gal	Galatians	Heb	Hebrews
Eph	Ephesians	James	James

Apocrypha

9 before Christmas

YEAR 1	Psalm	OT/1st Reading	NT/2nd Reading	Gospel
Communion	104.1–10; 29	Gen 1.1–3, 24–31a	Col 1.15–20	John 1.1–14
Morning Prayer	104 or 104.1–25	Prov 8.1, 22–31	Rev 21.1–7, 22–end	
Evening Prayer	148, 150	Gen 2.4b–end	John 3.1–12	
YEAR 2				
Communion		Gen 2.4b–9, 15–end	Rev 4	John 3.1–8
Morning Prayer		Job 38.1–21; 42.1–6	Acts 14.8–17	
Evening Prayer		Gen 1.1–2.3	John 1.1–14 (or –18)	

8 before Christmas

YEAR 1	Psalm	OT/1st Reading	NT/2nd Reading	Gospel
Communion	130; 10.13–end	Gen 4.1–10	1 John 3.9–18	Mark 7.14–23
Morning Prayer	25	Isa 44.6–22	1 Cor 10.1–13 (or –24)	
Evening Prayer	139.1–18	Gen 3	Rom 7.7–end	
YEAR 2				
Communion		Gen 3.1–15	Rom 7.7–13	John 3.13–21
Morning Prayer		Jer 17.5–14	Rom 5.12–end	
Evening Prayer		Exod 20.1–20	Mark 7.1–23	

7 before Christmas

YEAR 1	Psalm	OT/1st Reading	NT/2nd Reading	Gospel
Communion	1; 105.1–11	Gen 12.1–9	Rom 4.13–end	John 8.51–end
Morning Prayer	32, 36	Gen 18.1–19	Rom 9.1–13	
Evening Prayer	135 or 136	Isa 41.8–20	Matt 21.28–43	
YEAR 2				
Communion		Gen 22.1–18	James 2.14–24 (25, 26)	Luke 20.9–17
Morning Prayer		Isa 55	Gal 3.1–14	
Evening Prayer		Gen 13	John 8.31–end	

6 before Christmas

YEAR 1	Psalm	OT/1st Reading	NT/2nd Reading	Gospel
Communion	135.1–6; 77.11–end	Exod 3.7–15	Heb 3.1–6	John 6.25–35
Morning Prayer	66	Deut 18.15–end	Acts 3	
Evening Prayer	106.1–15, 42–end	Exod 6.2–13	Mark 13.1–13	
YEAR 2				
Communion		Exod 6.2–8	Heb 11.17–31	Mark 13.5–13
Morning Prayer		Exod 1.8–14, 22–2.10	Heb 3	
Evening Prayer		Exod 2.23–3.20	John 6.24–40	

5 before Christmas

YEAR 1	Psalm	OT/1st Reading	NT/2nd Reading	Gospel
Communion	80.1–7; 80.8–end	1 Kings 19.9–18	Rom 11.13–24	Matt 24.37–44
Morning Prayer	147	Gen 18.20–end	Mark 13.14–end	
Evening Prayer	75, 76	Jer 18.1–17	Rom 9.19–28	
YEAR 2				
Communion		Isa 10.20–23	Rom 9.19–28	Mark 13.14–23
Morning Prayer		Gen 6.5–end	1 Pet 3.8–end	
Evening Prayer		Jer 5.1–19	Rom 11.1–24	

Advent 1

YEAR 1	Psalm	OT/1st Reading	NT/2nd Reading	Gospel
Communion	50.1–6; 82	Isa 52.7–10	1 Thess 5.1–11	Luke 21.25–33
Morning Prayer	18.1–32	Isa 1.1–20	Luke 12.35–48	
Evening Prayer	68.1–20	Josh 7	Matt 25.31–end	
YEAR 2				
Communion		Isa 51.4–11	Rom 13.8–end	Matt 25.31–end
Morning Prayer		Isa 2.10–end	Matt 24.1–28	
Evening Prayer		Isa 52.1–12	1 Thess 5	

Advent 2

YEAR 1	Psalm	OT/1st Reading	NT/2nd Reading	Gospel
Communion	19.7–end; 119.129–136	Isa 55.1–11	2 Tim 3.14–4.5	John 5.36b–end
Morning Prayer	119.137–152	1 Kings 22.1–28	Rom 10.5–17	
Evening Prayer	119.89–104	Amos 8.4–12	Luke 4.14–30	
YEAR 2				
Communion		Isa 64.1–7	Rom 15.4–13	Luke 4.14–21
Morning Prayer		Jer 36.9–end (or –26)	Matt 25.14–30	
Evening Prayer		1 Sam 28.3–20	2 Tim 3.14–4.8	

Advent 3

YEAR 1	Psalm	OT/1st Reading	NT/2nd Reading	Gospel
Communion	126; Benedictus	Isa 40.1–11	1 Cor 4.1–5	John 1.19–28
Morning Prayer	80	Amos 7	Luke 1.1–25	
Evening Prayer	11, 14	Mal 3.1–5; 4	Matt 11.2–19 or	
			Phil 4.4–end	

YEAR 2

Communion	Mal 3.1–5	Phil 4.4–9	Matt 11.2–15
Morning Prayer	1 Kings 18.17–39	Luke 3.1–20	
Evening Prayer	Isa 40.1–11	1 Cor 3	

Advent 4

YEAR 1	Psalm	OT/1st Reading	NT/2nd Reading	Gospel
Communion	45.10–end; Magnificat	Isa 11.1–9	1 Cor 1.26–end	Luke 1.26–38a
Morning Prayer	40	1 Sam 1.1–20	Luke 1.39–55	
Evening Prayer	113, 123, 131	Zech 2	Rev 20.11–21.7	
YEAR 2				
Communion		Zech 2.10–end	Rev 21.1–7	Matt 1.18–23
Morning Prayer		Jer 33.10–16	Rev 22.6–end	
Evening Prayer		Isa 10.33–11.10	Luke 1.26–38a	

Christmas Eve

YEARS 1/2	Psalm	OT/1st Reading	NT/2nd Reading	Gospel
Communion	89.1–7 (8–18); 89.19–30	Isa 62.1–5	Acts 13.16–26	Luke 1.67–79
Morning Prayer	137, 138	Isa 58	Rom 1.1–7	
Evening Prayer	85	Isa 32.1–8	John 13.1–17	

Christmas Day

YEARS 1/2	Psalm	OT/1st Reading	NT/2nd Reading	Gospel
Communion	85; 96; 98	Isa 9.2, 6, 7	Titus 2.11–14; 3.3–7	Luke 2.1–14 (15–20)
		Isa 62.10–12	Heb 1.1–5 (6–12)	Luke 2.8–20
		Micah 5.2–4	1 John 4.7–14	John 1.1–14
Morning Prayer	19	Isa 35	John 3.16–21	
Evening Prayer	8, 110	Isa 65.17–end	1 John 1.1–9	

Christmas 1

YEAR 1	Psalm	OT/1st Reading	NT/2nd Reading	Gospel
Communion	2; 116.11–18	Isa 7.10–14	Gal 4.1–7	John 1.14–18
Morning Prayer	132	Isa 40.18–end	Col 1.1–20	
Evening Prayer	84, 122	Isa 12	Phil 2.1–11	
YEAR 2				
Communion		1 Sam 1.20–end	Rom 12.1–8	Luke 2.22–40
Morning Prayer		Haggai 2.1–9	1 Pet 2.1–10 or Luke 2.41–end	
Evening Prayer		Ruth 2.1–20a; 4.13–17	Rom 1.1–17	

Christmas 2

YEAR 1	Psalm	OT/1st Reading	NT/2nd Reading	Gospel
Communion	27.1–8; Nunc Dimmittis	Eccles 3.2–7 or Exod 12.21–27	Rom 8.11–17	Luke 2.41–end
Morning Prayer	89.19–38	Isa 43.1–13	Matt 2	
Evening Prayer	85, 87	1 Sam 1	John 4.19–26	
YEAR 2				
Communion		Isa 60.1–6	Rev 21.22–22.5	Matt 2.1–12, 19–23
Morning Prayer		Isa 46.3–end	Rom 15.8–21	
Evening Prayer		Isa 60.13–end	1 Cor 2	

Epiphany of our Lord

YEARS 1/2	Psalm	OT/1st Reading	NT/2nd Reading	Gospel
Communion	72.1–8; 72.10–end	Isa 49.1–6	Eph 3.1–12	Matt 2.1–12
Morning Prayer	2, 8	Isa 42.1–9	John 1.29–34	
Evening Prayer	96, 97	Isa 49.7–13	John 2.1–11	

Epiphany 1

YEAR 1	Psalm	OT/1st Reading	NT/2nd Reading	Gospel
Communion	36.5–10; 89.19–30	1 Sam 16.1–13a	Acts 10.34–38a	Matt 3.13–end
Morning Prayer	46, 47	Isa 61	Eph 2.1–10	
Evening Prayer	29, 30	Josh 3	Mark 1.1–13	
YEAR 2				
Communion		Isa 42.1–7	Eph 2.1–10	John 1.29–34
Morning Prayer		Gen 8.15–9.17	Acts 18.24–19.6	
Evening Prayer		1 Sam 16.1–13a	Matt 3	

Epiphany 2

YEAR 1	Psalm	OT/1st Reading	NT/2nd Reading	Gospel
Communion	100; 145.1–12	Jer 1.4–10	Acts 26.1, 9–20	Mark 1.14–20
Morning Prayer	15, 16	Ezek 2.1–7; 3.4–11	Matt 10.1–22	
Evening Prayer	121, 126	1 Sam 3.1–4.1a	John 1.35–end	
YEAR 2				
Communion		1 Sam 3.1–10	Gal 1.11–end	John 1.35–end
Morning Prayer		1 Kings 20.1–29	Matt 13.44–end	
Evening Prayer		Jer 1.4–end	Luke 5.1–11	

Epiphany 3

Year 1	Psalm	OT/1st Reading	NT/2nd Reading	Gospel
Communion	46; 107.1–9	Exod 33.12–end	1 John 1.1–7	John 2.1–11
Morning Prayer	135 or 136	Isa 26.1–9	John 4.43–end	
Evening Prayer	33	Deut 8.1–10	John 6.1–21	
Year 2				
Communion		Deut 8.1–6	Phil 4.10–20	John 6.1–14
Morning Prayer		Neh 13.15–22	John 5.1–21	
Evening Prayer		Exod 33.7–end	John 2.1–11	

Epiphany 4

Year 1	Psalm	OT/1st Reading	NT/2nd Reading	Gospel
Communion	48.9–end	1 Kings 8.22–30	1 Cor 3.10–17	John 2.13–22
Morning Prayer	34	Zech 8.1–17	Acts 15.1–21	
Evening Prayer	50	Exod 19.10–end	Heb 12.14–end	
Year 2				
Communion		Jer 7.1–11	Heb 12.18–end	John 4.19–26
Morning Prayer		1 Sam 21.1–6	Matt 12.1–21	
Evening Prayer		1 Kings 8.22–34; 9.1–3	John 2.13–end	

Epiphany 5

Years 1/2	Psalm	OT/1st Reading	NT/2nd Reading	Gospel
Communion	36; 49.1–12	Prov 2.1–9 / Ecclus 42.15–end	1 Cor 3.18–end	Matt 12.38–42
Morning Prayer	119.121–136	Jer 10.1–16 or Wisdom 7.28–8.9	1 Tim 3.14–4.10	
Evening Prayer	92	Job 12 or Ecclus 43.13–end	1 Cor 1.18–2.5	

Epiphany 6

Years 1/2	Psalm	OT/1st Reading	NT/2nd Reading	Gospel
Communion	43; 25.1–10	2 Sam 12.1–10	Rom 1.18–25	Matt 13.24–30
Morning Prayer	127, 128, 133	Isa 5.1–7 (or –16)	John 15.1–11	
Evening Prayer	75, 76	Prov 1.20–end	James 3	

9 before Easter

YEAR 1	Psalm	OT/1st Reading	NT/2nd Reading	Gospel
Communion	103.1–13; 34.11–18	Isa 30.18–21	1 Cor 4.8–13	Matt 5.1–12
Morning Prayer	71	Deut 5.1–21	Luke 13.22–end	
Evening Prayer	73	Prov 3.1–18	Mark 4.1–20	
YEAR 2				
Communion		Prov 3.1–8	1 Cor 2.1–10	Luke 8.4b–15
Morning Prayer		Job 28 (or 9–end)	Luke 6.20–38	
Evening Prayer		Isa 30.8–21	Matt 4.23–5.12	

8 before Easter

YEAR 1	Psalm	OT/1st Reading	NT/2nd Reading	Gospel
Communion	147.1–11; 131	Zeph 3.14–end	James 5.13–16a	Mark 2.1–12
Morning Prayer	139.1–18	2 Kings 4.8–37	Mark 1.21–end	
Evening Prayer	137.1–6; 146	2 Kings 5	Mark 7.24–end;	
		(or 1–14)	8.22–26	
YEAR 2				
Communion		2 Kings 5.1–14	2 Cor 12.1–10	Mark 7.24–end
Morning Prayer		Num 21.4–9	John 9 (or 9.1–25)	
Evening Prayer		2 Kings 20	Mark 5.1–20	

7 before Easter

YEAR 1	Psalm	OT/1st Reading	NT/2nd Reading	Gospel
Communion	32; 119.65–72	Hosea 14.1–7	Philemon 1–16	Mark 2.13–17
Morning Prayer	56, 57	Jer 33.1–11	Luke 7.36–8.3	
Evening Prayer	103	Num 15.27–36	John 8.1–11	
YEAR 2				
Communion		Num 15.32–36	Col 1.18–23	John 8.2–11
Morning Prayer		Jer 30.1–3, 10–22	Luke 13.1–17	
Evening Prayer		Hosea 14	Philemon	

Lent 1

YEAR 1	Psalm	OT/1st Reading	NT/2nd Reading	Gospel
Communion	119.1–8; 91.1–12	Gen 2.7–9; 3.1–7	Heb 2.14–end	Matt 4.1–11
Morning Prayer	119.9–24	1 Sam 26	Luke 22.1–23	
Evening Prayer	51	Deut 6	Heb 4	

Year 2

		OT/1st Reading	NT/2nd Reading	Gospel
Communion		Gen 4.1–10	Heb 4.12–end	Luke 4.1–13
Morning Prayer		Exod 17.1–13	Matt 26.1–30	
Evening Prayer		Deut 30.11–end	Heb 2.5–end	

Lent 2

Year 1	Psalm	OT/1st Reading	NT/2nd Reading	Gospel
Communion	119.33–40; 18.18–26	Gen 6.11–end	1 John 4.1–6	Luke 19.41–end
Morning Prayer	119.73–88	Gen 37.1–28	Luke 22.24–53 (or 39–53)	
Evening Prayer	74	Isa 35	Luke 11.14–26	
Year 2				
Communion		Gen 7.17–end	1 John 3.1–10	Matt 12.22–32
Morning Prayer		Amos 3	Matt 26.31–56	
Evening Prayer		2 Kings 6.8–23	Luke 19.41–20.8	

Lent 3

Year 1	Psalm	OT/1st Reading	NT/2nd Reading	Gospel
Communion	119.97–104; 115.1–7	Gen 22.1–13	Col 1.24–end	Luke 9.18–27
Morning Prayer	119.105–120	Exod 5.1–6.1	Luke 22.54–end	
Evening Prayer	31	Isa 45.14–end	Acts 12.1–17a	
Year 2				
Communion		Gen 12.1–9	1 Pet 2.19–end	Matt 16.13–end
Morning Prayer		Job 2	Matt 26.57–end	
Evening Prayer		Isa 59.9–20	Col 1.24–2.7	

Lent 4

Year 1	Psalm	OT/1st Reading	NT/2nd Reading	Gospel
Communion	119.153–160; 18.27–38	Exod 34.29–end	2 Cor 3.4–end	Luke 9.28–36
Morning Prayer	119.161–176	Exod 24	Luke 23.1–25	
Evening Prayer	23, 27	1 Kings 19.1–18	2 Pet 1.1–19	
Year 2				
Communion		Exod 3.1–6	2 Pet 1.16–19	Matt 17.1–13
Morning Prayer		Isa 52.13–53.6	Matt 27.1–32	
Evening Prayer		Exod 34.1–5, 29–end	2 Cor 3	

Lent 5

Year 1	Psalm	OT/1st Reading	NT/2nd Reading	Gospel
Communion	76.1–9; 22.23–29	Exod 6.2–13	Col 2.8–15	John 12.20–32
Morning Prayer	66	Lam 3.19–33	Luke 23.26–49	
Evening Prayer	130, 143.1–11	Jer 31.27–37	Mark 10.32–45	

YEAR 2

Communion	Jer 31.31–34	Heb 9.11–14	Mark 10.32–45
Morning Prayer	Isa 53.7–end	Matt 27.33–54	
Evening Prayer	Isa 63.1–16	John 12.20–36a	

Palm Sunday

YEARS 1/2	Psalm	OT/1st Reading	NT/2nd Reading	Gospel
Communion	22.1–11; 69.1–9 or	Isa 50.4–9a	Phil 2.5–11	Mark 14.32–15.41
	24; 45.1–7	Zech 9.9–12	1 Cor 1.18–25	Matt 21.1–13
Morning Prayer	61, 62	Jer 7.1–11 and	Luke 19.29–end	
		or Exod 11 and	Mark 14	
Evening Prayer	22.1–22	Isa 5.1–7	Mark 12.1–12	

Good Friday

YEARS 1/2	Psalm	OT/1st Reading	NT/2nd Reading	Gospel
Communion	22.14–22; 69.17–23	Isa 52.13–53 end	Heb 10.1–25	John 18.1–19.37
			Heb 10.12–22	John 19.1–37
			Heb 4.14–16; 5.7–9	
Morning Prayer	40 or 40.1–14	Gen 22.1–18	John 18 or	
			Mark 15.21–41	
Evening Prayer	130, 143.1–11	Lam 5.15–end	John 19.38–end or	
			Col 1.18–23	

Easter Eve

YEARS 1/2	Psalm	OT/1st Reading	NT/2nd Reading	Gospel
Communion	16.8–end; 23	Job 14.1–14	1 Pet 3.17–end	Matt 27.57–end
				John 2.18–22
Morning Prayer	142	Hosea 6.1–6	1 Pet 4.1–6	
Evening Prayer	116	Job 19.21–27	1 John 5.5–12	

Easter Day

YEARS 1/2	Psalm	OT/1st Reading	NT/2nd Reading	Gospel
Communion	118.14–24; 114	Isa 12	Rev 1.10–18	Matt 28.1–10
	Easter Anthems	Exod 14.15–22	1 Cor 15.12–20	John 20.1–10
				(or –18)
	Te Deum	Isa 43.16–21	Col 3.1–11	Mark 16.1–8
Morning Prayer	113, 114, 117	Isa 12	Rom 6.3–14	
Evening Prayer	118	Exod 14.5–end	John 20.11–23	

Easter 1

YEAR 1	Psalm	OT/1st Reading	NT/2nd Reading	Gospel
Communion	145.1–12; 34.1–10	Exod 15.1–11	1 Pet 1.3–9	John 20.19–29
Morning Prayer	30, 48	Deut 11.1–15	2 Cor 4.5–end	
Evening Prayer	115	Exod 16.1–15	John 6.24–51	
YEAR 2				
Communion		Exod 16.2–15	1 Cor 15.53–end	John 6.32–40
Morning Prayer		Deut 4.25–40	Rev 2.1–11	
Evening Prayer		Isa 51.1–16	John 20.24–end	

Easter 2

YEAR 1	Psalm	OT/1st Reading	NT/2nd Reading	Gospel
Communion	111; 23	Isa 25.6–9	Rev 19.6–9	Luke 24.13–35
Morning Prayer	49.1–16	Exod 32.1–14, 30–end	Luke 7.11–17	
Evening Prayer	2, 8	Ezek 34.1–16	John 10.1–18 or 1 Pet 5	
YEAR 2				
Communion		Ezek 34.7–16	1 Pet 5.1–11	John 10.7–16
Morning Prayer		Ezra 1.1–18	Rev 2.12–end	
Evening Prayer		Isa 25.1–9	Luke 24.13–35	

Easter 3

YEAR 1	Psalm	OT/1st Reading	NT/2nd Reading	Gospel
Communion	16; 30	Isa 61.1–7	1 Cor 15.1–11	John 21.1–14
Morning Prayer	121, 126	Num 22.1–35 (or 1–20)	Acts 17.16–end	
Evening Prayer	18.1–32	1 Kings 17.8–end	John 11.17–44	
YEAR 2				
Communion		1 Kings 17.17–end	Col 3.1–11	John 11.17–27
Morning Prayer		Ezra 3	Rev 3.1–13	
Evening Prayer		Num 13.1–2, 17–end	John 21.1–14	

Easter 4

YEAR 1	Psalm	OT/1st Reading	NT/2nd Reading	Gospel
Communion	33.1–12; 37.23–32	Isa 62.1–5	Rev 3.14–end	John 21.15–22
Morning Prayer	57, 63.1–9	Num 22.36–23.12	Luke 16.19–end	
Evening Prayer	77	Prov 4.1–18	2 Cor 4.13–5.15	

[TableStart]

Year 2

	Psalm	OT/1st Reading	NT/2nd Reading	Gospel
Communion		Prov 4.10–19	2 Cor 4.13–5.5	John 14.1–11
Morning Prayer		Neh 1	1 Cor 15.1–28	
Evening Prayer		Isa 62	John 21.15–end	

Easter 5

Year 1	Psalm	OT/1st Reading	NT/2nd Reading	Gospel
Communion	84; 15	Hosea 6.1–6	1 Cor 15.21–28	John 16.25–end
Morning Prayer	65, 67	Deut 28.1–14	Luke 10.38–11.13	
Evening Prayer	107.1–32	Deut 34	John 16.12–24	
Year 2				
Communion		Deut 34	Rom 8.28–end	John 16.12–24
Morning Prayer		Neh 2	Matt 13.24–43	
Evening Prayer		Hosea 6.1–6	1 Cor 15.35–end	

Ascension Day

Years 1/2	Psalm	OT/1st Reading	NT/2nd Reading	Gospel
Communion	8; 21.1–7	Dan 7.9–14	Acts 1.1–11	Matt 28.16–end
Morning Prayer	96, 97	2 Sam 23.1–5	Heb 1.1–2.4	
Evening Prayer	15, 24	Isa 52.7–12	Heb 2.5–end	

Sunday After Ascension Day

Year 1	Psalm	OT/1st Reading	NT/2nd Reading	Gospel
Communion	24; 47	Dan 7.9–14	Eph 1.15–end	Luke 24.45–end
Morning Prayer	108, 110	Isa 65.17–end	Rev 5	
Evening Prayer	138, 150	2 Kings 2.1–15	John 17 (or 1–13)	
Year 2				
Communion		2 Kings 2.1–15	Eph 4.1–13	Luke 24.45–end
Morning Prayer		Jer 31.1–13	Phil 2.1–18	
Evening Prayer		Dan 7.9–14	Eph 1.15–end	

Pentecost

Years 1/2	Psalm	OT/1st Reading	NT/2nd Reading	Gospel
Communion	122; 36.5–10	Gen 11.1–9 or Exod 19.16–25	Acts 2.1–11 or Acts 2.1–21	John 14.15–26 or John 20.19–23
Morning Prayer	68.1–20	Joel 2.21–end	Rom 8.1–17	
Evening Prayer	104, or 104.1–5, 26–end	Ezek 37.1–14	Rom 8.18–27	

Pentecost 1 – Trinity Sunday

YEARS 1/2	Psalm	OT/1st Reading	NT/2nd Reading	Gospel
Communion	93; 97	Isa 6.1–8	Eph 1.3–14	John 14.8–17
Morning Prayer	29, 33	Exod 34.1–10	Acts 2.22–36	
Evening Prayer	145	Isa 40.12–end	Mark 1.1–13	

Pentecost 2

YEAR 1	Psalm	OT/1st Reading	NT/2nd Reading	Gospel
Communion	95.1–7; 135.1–6	Exod 19.1–6	1 Pet 2.1–10	John 15.1–5
Morning Prayer	85, 133	Deut 30.1–10	Matt 18.10–22	
Evening Prayer	89.1–18	2 Sam 7.1–17	Luke 14.7–24	
YEAR 2				
Communion		2 Sam 7.4–16	Acts 2.37–end	Luke 14.15–24
Morning Prayer		Ezek 37.15–end	Eph 2.11–end	
Evening Prayer		Exod 19.1–11	1 Pet 2.1–10	

Pentecost 3

YEAR 1	Psalm	OT/1st Reading	NT/2nd Reading	Gospel
Communion	44.1–9; 150	Deut 6.17–end	Rom 6.3–11	John 15.5–11
Morning Prayer	11, 20	Micah 3.5–end	Matt 5.27–end	
Evening Prayer	32, 36	Deut 5.1–21	Acts 4.1–22	
YEAR 2				
Communion		Deut 8.11–end	Acts 4.8–12	Luke 8.41–end
Morning Prayer		Isa 32.1–8	Mark 4.21–end	
Evening Prayer		Deut 6.10–end	Acts 23.11–24	

Pentecost 4

YEAR 1	Psalm	OT/1st Reading	NT/2nd Reading	Gospel
Communion	63.1–9; 67	Deut 7.6–11	Gal 3.23–4.7	John 15.12–17
Morning Prayer	42, 43	Ezek 18.1–4, 19–end	Rom 14.1–15.3	
Evening Prayer	147	Josh 24.1–5, 13–31	Acts 8.26–end	
YEAR 2				
Communion		Isa 63.7–14	Acts 8.26–38	Luke 15.1–10
Morning Prayer		1 Kings 10.1–13	John 4.1–26 (or 1–42)	
Evening Prayer		Deut 7.1–11	John 15.12–end	

Pentecost 5

Year 1	Psalm	OT/1st Reading	NT/2nd Reading	Gospel
Communion	119.57–64; 119.89–96	Exod 20.1–17	Eph 5.1–10	Matt 19.16–26
Morning Prayer	119.41–56	Neh 8.1–12	Luke 11.37–end	
Evening Prayer	67, 98	2 Kings 6.24, 25; 7.3–end	Acts 11.1–18	
Year 2				
Communion		Ruth 1.8–17, 22	Acts 11.4–18	Luke 10.1–12
Morning Prayer		Jonah 3 & 4	Acts 13.1–13	
Evening Prayer		Exod 20.1–20	Matt 19.16–end	

Pentecost 6

Year 1	Psalm	OT/1st Reading	NT/2nd Reading	Gospel
Communion	112; 1	Exod 24.3–11	Col 3.12–17	Luke 15.11–end
Morning Prayer	77	Isa 43.14–44.5	Mark 2.18–3.6	
Evening Prayer	102	Dan 1	Eph 4.17–end	
Year 2				
Communion		Micah 6.1–8	Eph 4.17–end	Mark 10.46–end
Morning Prayer		2 Sam 12.1–18a (or –23)	Acts 9.1–22	
Evening Prayer		2 Kings 22	Luke 15.1–10	

Pentecost 7

Year 1	Psalm	OT/1st Reading	NT/2nd Reading	Gospel
Communion	62; 103.8–18	Hosea 11.1–9	1 Cor 12.27–13 end	Matt 18.21–end
Morning Prayer	81	Gen 50.15–end	1 John 2.1–17	
Evening Prayer	99, 100, 101	Deut 10.12–11.1	Mark 12.28–end	
Year 2				
Communion		Deut 10.12–11.1	Rom 8.1–11	Mark 12.28–34
Morning Prayer		Deut 24.10–end	1 John 3.13–end	
Evening Prayer		Hosea 11.1–9	1 Cor 12.27–13 end	

Pentecost 8

Year 1	Psalm	OT/1st Reading	NT/2nd Reading	Gospel
Communion	25.1–10; 27.1–8	Ezek 36.24–28	Gal 5.16–25	John 15.16–end
Morning Prayer	73	Num 11.16–17, 24–29	Acts 8.4–25	
Evening Prayer	91	Isa 32.9–18	1 Cor 12.1–31a	

Year 2

Communion	Ezek 37.1–14	1 Cor 12.4–13	Luke 6.27–38
Morning Prayer	Prov 8.1–17	Luke 6.39–end	
Evening Prayer	Exod 35.20–36.7	1 Cor 14.1–19	

Pentecost 9

Year 1	Psalm	OT/1st Reading	NT/2nd Reading	Gospel
Communion	18.1–7; 18.32–38	Josh 1.1–9	Eph 6.10–20	John 17.11b–19
Morning Prayer	90	Neh 4.7–end	Matt 6.1–18	
Evening Prayer	24, 46	1 Sam 17.1–11, 32–51	2 Cor 6.1–10	

Year 2				
Communion		1 Sam 17.37–50	2 Cor 6.3–10	Mark 9.14–29
Morning Prayer		2 Sam 1.1–12, 17–end	1 Tim 6.6–end	
Evening Prayer		Num 6.1–5, 22–end	Eph 6.10–end	

Pentecost 10

Year 1	Psalm	OT/1st Reading	NT/2nd Reading	Gospel
Communion	71.1–8; 73.23–end	Job 42.1–6	Phil 2.1–11	John 13.1–15
Morning Prayer	19	1 Sam 18.1–16	Mark 9.30–end	
Evening Prayer	1, 4	1 Sam 24.1–17	Gal 6	

Year 2				
Communion		1 Sam 24.9–17 (or 1–17)	Gal 6.1–10	Luke 7.36–end
Morning Prayer		2 Sam 9	Matt 6.19–end	
Evening Prayer		Job 38; 42.1–6 or Job 38.1–11; 42.1–6	John 13.1–20	

Pentecost 11

Year 1	Psalm	OT/1st Reading	NT/2nd Reading	Gospel
Communion	31.21–end; 40.1–7	Isa 42.1–7	2 Cor 4.1–10	John 13.31–35
Morning Prayer	123, 124, 125	Exod 18.13–26	Acts 6	
Evening Prayer	82, 112	1 Chron 29.1–16	Luke 17.5–10	

Year 2				
Communion		1 Chron 29.1–9	Phil 1.1–11	Matt 20.1–16
Morning Prayer		1 Kings 12.1–20	2 Cor 9	
Evening Prayer		Isa 42.1–12	John 13.21–end	

Pentecost 12

YEAR 1	Psalm	OT/1st Reading	NT/2nd Reading	Gospel
Communion	96.1–6; 96.7–end	Isa 49.1–6	2 Cor 5.14–6.2	John 17.20–end
Morning Prayer	145, 150	Ezek 33.1–9, 30–end	Acts 16.1–15	
Evening Prayer	34	Jonah 1 & 2	Acts 28 (or 11–end)	
YEAR 2				
Communion		Micah 4.1–5	Acts 17.22–end	Matt 5.13–16
Morning Prayer		Amos 5.14–24 (or 6–24)	Rom 15.14–29	
Evening Prayer		Isa 49.1–13	2 Cor 5.11–6.2	

Pentecost 13

YEAR 1	Psalm	OT/1st Reading	NT/2nd Reading	Gospel
Communion	31.1–5; 43	Isa 50.4–9a	Acts 7.54–8.1	John 16.1–11
Morning Prayer	130, 137.1–6	2 Kings 19.8–19	Acts 16.16–end	
Evening Prayer	22.1–22	Jer 20.1–11a	Acts 20.17–end	
YEAR 2				
Communion		Jer 20.7–11a	Acts 20.17–35	Matt 10.16–22
Morning Prayer		Isa 49.13–23	Matt 11.20–end	
Evening Prayer		Isa 50.4–9a	1 Pet 4	

Pentecost 14

YEAR 1	Psalm	OT/1st Reading	NT/2nd Reading	Gospel
Communion	127; 128	Prov 31.10–end	Eph 5.25–6.4	Mark 10.2–16
Morning Prayer	103	Gen 29.1–20	2 Tim 1.1–14	
Evening Prayer	45	Gen 45 (or 1–15)	Luke 2.41–end	
YEAR 2				
Communion		Gen 45.1–15	Eph 3.14–end	Luke 11. 1–13
Morning Prayer		Gen 47.1–12	Col 3.12–21	
Evening Prayer		Prov 31.10–end	1 Cor 1.1–18	

Pentecost 15

YEAR 1	Psalm	OT/1st Reading	NT/2nd Reading	Gospel
Communion	82; 20	Isa 45.1–7	Rom 13.1–7	Matt 22.15–22
Morning Prayer	50	Dan 5	Acts 25.1–12	
Evening Prayer	72	1 Kings 3.4–15 (or 5–end)	1 Tim 1.12–2.8	

YEAR 2

Communion		1 Kings 3.4–15	1 Tim 2.1–7	Matt 14.1–12
Morning Prayer		1 Sam 8.4–22a	1 Pet 2.11–end	
Evening Prayer		Isa 45.1–13	Matt 22.1–33	

Pentecost 16

YEAR 1	Psalm	OT/1st Reading	NT/2nd Reading	Gospel
Communion	34.1–10; 34.11–18	Lev 19.9–18	Rom 12.9–end	Luke 10.25–37
Morning Prayer	107.1–32	1 Kings 21 (or 1–23)	Matt 7.1–12	
Evening Prayer	41, 133	Deut 15.1–18	1 John 4.7–end	
YEAR 2				
Communion		Deut 15.7–11	1 John 4.15–end	Luke 16.19–end
Morning Prayer		Prov 25.6–22	James 2.1–13	
Evening Prayer		Lev 19.1–4, 9–18	Luke 10.25–37	

Pentecost 17

YEAR 1	Psalm	OT/1st Reading	NT/2nd Reading	Gospel
Communion	56; 57	Jer 7.1–11	James 1.16–end	Luke 17.11–19
Morning Prayer	91, 93	Judges 7.1–8, 19–23 (or 1–23)	John 7.1–24	
Evening Prayer	19, 20	Jer 32.1–15	Luke 14.25–end	
YEAR 2				
Communion		Jer 32.6–15	Gal 2.15–3.9	Luke 7.1–10
Morning Prayer		Josh 5.13–6.20	John 6.51–69	
Evening Prayer		Josh 14.6–14	Acts 19.21–end	

Pentecost 18

YEAR 1	Psalm	OT/1st Reading	NT/2nd Reading	Gospel
Communion	145.14–end; 90.13–end	Deut 26.1–11	2 Cor 8.1–9	Matt 5.17–26
Morning Prayer	118	Eccles 11 & 12	Luke 12.1–21	
Evening Prayer	116	Neh 6.1–16 or Ecclus 38.24–end	Rom 12	
YEAR 2				
Communion		Neh 6.1–16 or Ecclus 38.24–end	1 Pet 4.7–11	Matt 25.14–30
Morning Prayer		Jer 26.1–16	Phil 1.12–26	
Evening Prayer		Haggai 1	Matt 5.13–26	

Pentecost 19

YEAR 1	Psalm	OT/1st Reading	NT/2nd Reading	Gospel
Communion	139.1–11; 65.1–7	Gen 28.10–end	Heb 11.1, 2, 8–16	Matt 6.24–end
Morning Prayer	37.1–22	Job 23.1–12	2 Cor 1.1–22	
Evening Prayer	85, 111	Dan 6.1–23	Luke 18.35–19.10	
YEAR 2				
Communion		Dan 6.10–23	Rom 5.1–11	Luke 19.1–10
Morning Prayer		Josh 23	2 Cor 11.16–31	
Evening Prayer		Gen 28.10–end	Heb 11.1–16	

Pentecost 20

YEAR 1	Psalm	OT/1st Reading	NT/2nd Reading	Gospel
Communion	37.35–end	Dan 3.13–26	Rom 8.18–25	Luke 9.51–end
Morning Prayer	51	Job 1	2 Tim 2.1–19	
Evening Prayer	39	Gen 32.3–30	Acts 27.1–25 (or 13–25)	
YEAR 2				
Communion		Gen 32.22–30	1 Cor 9.19–end	Matt 7.13–27
Morning Prayer		Jer 38.1–13	James 1.1–15	
Evening Prayer		Dan 3	Heb 11.32–12.2	

Pentecost 21

YEAR 1	Psalm	OT/1st Reading	NT/2nd Reading	Gospel
Communion	126; 11	Hab 2.1–4	Acts 26.1–8	Luke 18.1–8
Morning Prayer	23, 24 or 78.1–24	Ezek 34.11–24	2 Pet 3	
Evening Prayer	15, 16	Ezek 12.21–end	1 Pet 1.3–21	
YEAR 2				
Communion		Ezek 12.21–end	1 Pet 1.13–21	John 11.17–22
Morning Prayer		Job 4.1 & 5.1–16	Heb 10.19–end	
Evening Prayer		Hab 2.1–14	Luke 18.1–14	

Pentecost 22

YEARS 1/2	Psalm	OT/1st Reading	NT/2nd Reading	Gospel
Communion	119.1–8; 112	Deut 11.18–28	1 John 2.22–end	Luke 16.1–9
Morning Prayer	42, 43	Prov 14.31–15.17	James 4.13–5.11	
Evening Prayer	40	Jer 6.16–21	Mark 3.7–end	

Pentecost 23

Year 1	Psalm	OT/1st Reading	NT/2nd Reading	Gospel
Communion	15; 146	Jer 29.1, 4–14	Phil 3.7–end	John 17.1–10
Morning Prayer	89.1–18	Dan 10.2–19	Rev 1.1–18	
Evening Prayer	84, 122	Isa 33.13–22	Matt 24.45–25.13	
Year 2				
Communion		Isa 33.17–22	Rev 7.2–4, 9–end	Matt 25.1–13
Morning Prayer		Ezek 11.14–21	Heb 13.1–21	
Evening Prayer		Jer 29.1–14	Phil 3.7–end	

CONVERSION TABLES

TABLE 1

HYMNS ANCIENT & MODERN REVISED: NEW STANDARD

AMR	NS	AMR	NS	AMR	NS	AMR	NS	AMR	NS
1		44		87		130	74	173	106
2		45	23	88		131		174	
3	1	46		89	57	132	75	175	107
4	2	47	24	90		133	76	176	108
5	3	48	25	91	55	134	77	177	109
6		49	26	92	56	135	78	178	110
7	4	50	27	93		136	79	179	111
8		51	28	94		137	80	180	
9		52	29	95		138		181	112
10		53	30	96	58	139	81	182	113
11		54	31	97	59	140	82	183	114
12		55	32	98	60	141	83	184	115
13		56		99	61	142	84	185	117
14		57		100		143		186	118
15	5	58	33	101		144		187	119
16	6	59	34	102	63	145		188	
17	7	60	35	103		146	86	189	120
18	8	61	36	104	64	147	87	190	121
19		62	37	105		148	88	191	
20	9	63	38	106	65	149		192	122
21		64	39	107	66	150		193	123
22		65	40	108	67	151		194	
23	10	66	41	109		152		195	124
24	11	67	42	110		153	89	196	125
25		68	43	111	68	154	90	197	126
26	12	69	44	112		155	91	198	127
27	13	70		113		156	92	199	128
28		71	45	114		157	93	200	129
29		72		115		158	94	201	
30	14	73		116		159		202	
31	15	74		117		160	95	203	
32		75	47	118	69	161	96	204	130
33	16	76	48	119		162		205	131
34	17	77	49	120		163		206	
35	18	78	50	121		164	97	207	132
36		79	51	122		165	99	208	133
37		80	52	123		166	100	209	
38		81	53	124		167	101	210	135
39		82		125		168		211	136
40	20	83		126		169	102	212	
41		84		127		170	103	213	
42	21	85		128	73	171	104	214	137
43	22	86		129		172	105	215	138

AMR = Hymns Ancient & Modern REVISED,
NS = Hymns Ancient & Modern NEW STANDARD

AMR	NS	AMR	NS	AMR	NS	AMR	NS	AMR	NS
216	139	265		314	226	363	250	412	272
217	140	266	180	315		364	251	413	
218	141	267		316		365	192	414	274
219	142	268		317	227	366	193	415	
220	143	269		318	228	367	194	416	275
221	144	270		319		368	195	417	276
222	145	271		320		369	196	418	
223	146	272	182	321		370	197	419	
224	147	273		322		371	198	420	
225	148	274	183	323		372	199	421	277
226	149	275		324	229	373	200	422	
227		276		325	230	374	201	423	273
228		277		326	231	375	202	424	
229	150	278	184	327	232	376	203	425	
230	151	279	185	328		377	204	426	
231	152	280		329	233	378		427	
232	153	281	186	330	234	379	205	428	
233	154	282	187	331	235	380	206	429	
234	155	283	188	332	236	381		430	
235	156	284	189	333	237	382	207	431	19
236	157	285	190	334		383	252	432	46
237	158	286	191	335	238	384	253	433	
238	159	287		336	239	385	254	434	
239		288	319	337	240	386		435	70
240		289	208	338		387	255	436	71
241		290	209	339		388		437	
242	160	291	210	340		389		438	
243	161	292	211	341	241	390	256	439	
244		293	212	342	242	391		440	
245	162	294		343	243	392		441	
246	163	295	213	344	244	393	257	442	116
247	164	296	214	345		394	258	443	
248	165	297		346		395		444	134
249		298	215	347	245	396	259	445	
250	166	299	216	348		397	260	446	
251	167	300	217	349	246	398	261	447	
252	168	301	218	350		399	262	448	320
253		302		351	247	400	263	449	
254	169	303	219	352		401	264	450	
255	170	304	220	353		402	265	451	
256	171	305		354		403	266	452	
257	172	306		355		404		453	
258	173	307	221	356		405	267	454	
259	174	308		357		406		455	
260	175	309	222	358		407	268	456	
261	176	310	223	359		408	269	457	
262	177	311	224	360	248	409	270	458	
263	178	312		361	249	410		459	279
264	179	313	225	362		411	271	460	

AMR	NS	AMR	NS	AMR	NS	AMR	NS	AMR	NS
461		497		532		569	322	605	
462		498		534		570	323	606	330
463	280	499		535		571	324	607	
464		500		536		572		608	
465		501		537		573		609	
466		502		538		574		610	
467		503	297	539		575		611	
468		504		540		576		612	
469	281	505		541	313	577	293	613	
470		506	298	542		578	294	614	
471		507	299	543		579	295	615	
472		508	300	544	314	580		616	
473	282	509		545		581		617	
474	283	510	301	546		582	296	618	
475		511		547		583		619	
476	284	512	309	548		584		620	332
477		513	310	549		585		621	
478	285	514	311	550		586		622	
479	286	515		551	315	587		623	
480	287	516		552	316	588		624	
481	288	517		553		589		625	
482	289	518		554		590		626	
483	290	519		555	317	591	325	627	
484	291	520		556		592		628	
485		521		557		593	326	629	333
486		522		558		594		630	98
487	292	523		559		595	327	631	331
488		524	302	560	318	596	54	632	
489		525	303	561		597	328	633	72
490		526	304	562		598		634	
491		527	305	563		599	62	635	
492		528	306	564	321	600		636	181
493		529		565		601			
494	278	530	307	566		602	329		
495		533	312	567		603	85		
496		531	308	568		604			

TABLE 2

HYMNS ANCIENT & MODERN NEW STANDARD:
100 HYMNS FOR TODAY: MORE HYMNS FOR TODAY

HT	NS	HT	NS	HT	NS	HT	NS	HT	NS
1	334	41	374	81	414	121	454	161	494
2	335	42	375	82	415	122	455	162	495
3	336	43	376	83	416	123	456	163	496
4	337	44	377	84	417	124	457	164	497
5	338	45	378	85	418	125	458	165	498
6	339	46	379	86	419	126	459	166	499
7	340	47	380	87	420	127	460	167	500
8	341	48	381	88	421	128	461	168	501
9	342	49	382	89	422	129	462	169	502
10	343	50	383	90	423	130	463	170	503
11	344	51	384	91	424	131	464	171	504
12	345	52	385	92	425	132	465	172	505
13	346	53	386	93	426	133	466	173	506
14	347	54	387	94	427	134	467	174	507
15	348	55	388	95	428	135	468	175	508
16	349	56	389	96	429	136	469	176	509
17	350	57	390	97	430	137	470	177	510
18	351	58	391	98	431	138	471	178	511
19	352	59	392	99	432	139	472	179	512
20	353	60	393	100	433	140	473	180	513
21	354	61	394	101	434	141	474	181	514
22	355	62	395	102	435	142	475	182	515
23	356	63	396	103	436	143	476	183	516
24	357	64	397	104	437	144	477	184	517
25	358	65	398	105	438	145	478	185	518
26	359	66	399	106	439	146	479	186	519
27	360	67	400	107	440	147	480	187	520
28	361	68	401	108	441	148	481	188	521
29	362	69	402	109	442	149	482	189	522
30	363	70	403	110	443	150	483	190	523
31	364	71	404	111	444	151	484	191	524
32	365	72	405	112	445	152	485	192	525
33	366	73	406	113	446	153	486	193	526
34	367	74	407	114	447	154	487	194	527
35	368	75	408	115	448	155	488	195	528
36	369	76	409	116	449	156	489	196	529
37	370	77	410	117	450	157	490	197	530
38	371	78	411	118	451	158	491	198	531
39	372	79	412	119	452	159	492	199	532
40	373	80	413	120	453	160	493	200	533

HT = 100 Hymns for Today, More Hymns for Today,
NS = Hymns Ancient & Modern NEW STANDARD

TABLE 3

SONGS AND HYMNS OF FELLOWSHIP

SOF	Book	SOF	Book	SOF	Book	SOF	Book	SOF	Book
1	1/1	41	H/13	81	2/178	121	2/191	161	3/376
2	H/1	42	2/171	82	3/353	122	2/192	162	2/205
3	3/331	43	3/341	83	3/354	123	H/25	163	1/37
4	2/160	44	1/8	84	3/355	124	2/193	164	3/377
5	2/161	45	1/9	85	3/356	125	H/26	165	3/378
6	2/162	46	H/14	86	2/179	126	3/369	166	2/206
7	H/2	47	H/15	87	3/357	127	3/370	167	3/379
8	H/3	48	2/172	88	H/21	128	2/194	168	H/35
9	2/163	49	3/342	89	2/180	129	3/371	169	3/380
10	H/4	50	1/10	90	2/181	130	2/195	170	3/381
11	2/164	51	3/343	91	3/358	131	3/372	171	3/382
12	H/5	52	1/11	92	3/359	132	2/196	172	1/38
13	3/332	53	3/334	93	2/182	133	3/373	173	1/39
14	3/333	54	H/16	94	1/21	134	H/27	174	3/383
15	H/6	55	1/12	95	2/183	135	H/28	175	1/40
16	H/7	56	2/173	96	3/360	136	2/197	176	1/41
17	H/8	57	1/13	97	3/361	137	1/28	177	2/207
18	2/165	58	1/14	98	1/22	138	3/374	178	H/36
19	1/2	59	2/174	99	2/184	139	1/29	179	3/384
20	1/3	60	1/15	100	3/362	140	2/198	180	2/208
21	3/334	61	1/16	101	2/185	141	2/199	181	3/385
22	3/335	62	2/175	102	1/23	142	2/200	182	2/209
23	1/4	63	3/345	103	H/22	143	H/29	183	H/37
24	2/166	64	H/17	104	H/23	144	H/30	184	3/386
25	3/336	65	3/346	105	1/24	145	H/31	185	H/38
26	H/9	66	3/347	106	2/186	146	H/32	186	2/210
27	3/337	67	1/18	107	3/363	147	1/30	187	1/42
28	2/167	68	2/176	108	2/187	148	2/201	188	1/43
29	2/168	69	3/348	109	1/25	149	2/202	189	1/44
30	2/169	70	3/349	110	3/364	150	1/31	190	1/45
31	H/10	71	3/350	111	3/365	151	H/33	191	3/387
32	3/338	72	1/17	112	2/188	152	1/32	192	2/211
33	3/339	73	1/18	113	2/189	153	H/34	193	1/46
34	2/170	74	3/351	114	1/26	154	2/203	194	1/47
35	1/5	75	H/19	115	3/366	155	1/33	195	2/212
36	H/11	76	H/20	116	2/190	156	1/34	196	H/39
37	3/340	77	1/19	117	1/27	157	2/204	197	1/48
38	H/12	78	1/20	118	H/24	158	1/35	198	2/213
39	1/6	79	2/177	119	3/367	159	1/36	199	3/388
40	1/7	80	3/352	120	3/368	160	3/375	200	H/40

SOF = Songs and Hymns of Fellowship, Book = Indicates music book and song number, 1/ = Book 1, 2/ = Book 2, 3/ = Book 3, H/ = Hymns of Fellowship.

SOF	Book	SOF	Book	SOF	Book	SOF	Book	SOF	Book
201	3/389	250	3/409	299	3/425	348	3/437	396	3/453
202	2/214	251	2/228	300	3/426	349	2/255	397	2/266
203	1/49	252	1/62	301	H/51	350	3/438	398	3/454
204	3/390	253	1/63	302	3/427	351	3/439	399	3/455
205	2/215	254	2/229	303	1/77	352	3/440	400	H/71
206	3/391	255	3/410	304	H/52	353	H/59	401	3/456
207	3/392	256	3/411	305	2/238	354	2/256	402	2/267
208	3/393	257	1/64	306	H/53	355	1/89	403	3/457
209	3/394	258	2/230	307	2/239	356	H/60	404	2/268
210	H/41	259	2/231	308	1/78	357	3/441	405	1/98
211	1/50	260	2/232	309	3/428	358	2/257	406	2/269
212	1/51	261	2/233	310	3/429	359	2/258	407	H/72
213	H/42	262	1/65	311	2/240	360	1/90	408	1/99
214	3/395	263	2/234	312	1/79	361	H/61	409	2/270
215	3/396	264	3/412	313	3/430	362	H/62	410	2/271
216	2/216	265	3/413	314	3/431	363	2/259	411	2/272
217	3/397	266	H/43	315	2/241	364	3/442	412	2/273
218	3/398	267	1/66	316	2/242	365	3/443	413	3/458
219	3/399	268	3/414	317	2/243	366	2/260	414	1/100
220	3/400	269	H/44	318	1/80	367	3/444	415	H/73
221	1/52	270	3/415	319	2/244	368	H/63	416	3/459
222	3/401	271	1/67	320	3/432	369	3/445	417	2/274
223	2/217	272	3/416	321	2/245	370	H/64	418	3/460
224	3/402	273	2/235	322	2/246	371	1/91	419	H/74
225	3/403	274	1/68	323	1/81	372	3/446	420	2/275
226	1/53	275	1/69	324	H/54	373	1/92	421	H/75
227	1/54	276	1/70	325	2/247	374	3/447	422	3/461
228	3/404	277	2/236	326	1/82	375	1/93	423	2/276
229	1/55	278	1/71	327	3/433	376	1/94	424	H/76
230	2/218	279	3/417	328	2/248	377	1/95	425	1/101
231	2/219	280	2/237	329	3/434	378	H/65	426	2/277
232	2/220	281	3/418	330	2/249	379	3/448	427	3/462
233	1/56	282	3/419	331	2/250	380	2/216	428	H/77
234	1/57	283	3/420	332	H/55	381	2/262	429	H/78
235	1/58	284	1/72	333	2/251	382	3/449	430	3/463
236	2/221	285	3/421	334	H/56	383	2/263	431	3/464
237	2/222	286	H/45	335	2/252	384	3/450	432	1/102
238	2/223	287	3/422	336	H/57	385	3/451	433	2/278
239	3/405	288	1/73	337	2/253	386	H/66	434	2/279
240	3/406	289	H/46	338	1/83	387	2/264	435	3/465
241	2/224	290	1/74	339	1/84	388	H/67	436	3/366
242	2/225	291	H/47	340	3/435	SOF	Book	437	3/467
243	1/59	292	1/75	341	1/85	389	3/452	438	2/280
244	1/60	293	1/76	342	H/58	390	2/265	439	H/79
245	3/407	294	H/48	343	1/86	391	1/96	440	3/468
246	3/408	295	H/49	344	2/254	392	H/68	441	H/80
247	2/226	296	H/50	345	1/87	393	H/69	442	3/469
248	1/61	297	3/423	346	3/436	394	H/70	443	3/470
249	2/227	298	3/424	347	1/88	395	1/97	444	2/282

SOF	Book	SOF	Book	SOF	Book	SOF	Book	SOF	Book
445	3/471	486	3/484	527	1/125	568	1/140	609	2/319
446	2/281	487	H/87	528	3/497	569	1/141	610	H/112
447	1/103	488	3/485	529	1/126	570	3/504	611	3/516
448	3/472	489	H/88	530	3/498	571	1/142	612	3/517
449	2/283	490	2/293	531	1/127	572	3/505	613	1/154
450	H/81	491	3/486	532	H/98	573	2/311	614	2/320
451	3/473	492	3/487	533	H/99	574	1/143	615	2/321
452	H/82	493	3/488	534	3/499	575	1/144	616	1/155
453	2/284	494	3/489	535	2/299	576	2/312	617	2/322
454	1/104	495	H/89	536	1/128	577	3/506	618	1/156
455	1/105	496	1/115	537	2/300	578	3/507	619	3/518
456	3/474	497	H/90	538	3/500	579	1/145	620	1/157
457	2/285	498	3/490	539	2/301	580	2/313	621	2/323
458	3/475	499	2/294	540	2/302	581	1/146	622	2/324
459	3/476	500	1/116	541	2/303	582	1/147	623	3/519
460	3/477	501	1/117	542	3/501	583	1/148	624	3/520
461	3/478	502	2/295	543	2/304	584	1/149	625	3/521
462	1/106	503	1/118	544	3/502	585	3/508	626	3/522
463	H/83	504	H/91	545	H/100	586	3/509	627	H/113
464	2/286	505	H/92	546	1/129	587	3/510	628	H/114
465	H/84	506	H/93	547	1/130	588	H/105	629	2/325
466	2/287	507	H/94	548	1/131	589	1/150	630	1/158
467	2/288	508	1/119	549	2/305	590	H/106	631	3/523
468	1/107	509	1/120	550	2/306	591	2/314	632	3/524
469	H/85	510	2/296	551	1/132	592	3/511	633	3/525
470	2/289	511	3/491	552	H/101	593	1/151	634	3/526
471	2/290	512	H/95	553	3/503	594	3/512	635	2/326
472	1/108	513	1/121	554	H/102	595	2/315	636	2/327
473	1/109	514	1/122	555	2/307	596	3/513	637	1/159
474	3/479	515	1/123	556	1/133	597	1/152	638	3/527
475	3/480	516	2/297	557	1/134	598	H/107	639	2/328
476	2/291	517	3/492	558	H/103	599	3/514	640	2/329
477	1/110	518	H/96	559	H/104	600	1/153	641	2/330
478	3/481	519	3/493	560	1/135	601	3/515	642	3/528
479	3/482	520	3/494	561	2/308	602	H/108	643	3/529
480	1/111	521	3/495	562	1/136	603	H/109	644	3/530
481	1/112	522	1/124	563	1/137	604	2/316	645	3/531
482	3/483	523	2/298	564	1/138	605	H/110		
483	H/86	524	3/496	565	2/309	606	2/317		
484	1/113	525	H/97	566	2/310	607	2/318		
485	2/292	526		567	1/139	608	H/111		

TABLE 4

SONGS INCLUDED ONLY IN
SONGS OF FELLOWSHIP 90/91

As we seek your face	1
Blessed be the name of the Lord	2
Come and see, come and see	3
Enter in to his great love	4
For you are my God	5
Give thanks to the Lord, call	6
Glory, honour, all power be to God	7
God of all comfort	8
Hear, O Lord, our cry	9
Holiness unto the Lord	10
Holy, holy, holy is the Lord	11
Holy One, Holy One	12
I come to you in Jesus' name	13
I exalt you, just and true	14
I lift my hands to the coming King	15
I will praise you with the harp	16
Jesus shall take the highest honour	17
Jesus, Jesus, holy and anointed One	18
Jesus, you are the power	19
Lord, how majestic you are	20
Lord, I raise my hands to bless you	21
Lord, your name is holy	22
Make us one, Lord	23
May my life (Sacrificial love)	24
My Lord, what love is this	25
Not unto us	27
Now unto the King	26
O Lord, you have been good	28
Only by grace can we enter	29
Our confidence is in the Lord	30
Peace like a river	31
The trumpets sound	32
Swing wide the gates	33
We are his children (Go forth)	34

TABLE 5

MISSION PRAISE COMBINED EDITION

IND	COMB	IND	COMB	IND	COMB	IND	COMB	IND	COMB
1	3	41	115	81	258	121	374	161	480
2	4	42	117	82	263	122	375	162	473
3	11	43	132	83	266	123	379	163	486
4	25	44	139	84	272	124	381	164	488
5	13	45	133	85	275	125	380	165	490
6	20	46	142	86	278	126	385	166	494
7	29	47	144	87	287	127	382	167	495
8	21	48	146	88	274	128	383	168	496
9	30	49	143	89	279	129	386	169	499
10	31	50	151	90	284	130	394	170	500
11	33	51	148	91	285	131	388	171	515
12	36	52	153	92	288	132	396	172	501
13	38	53	158	93	304	133	401	173	506
14	40	54	163	94	295	134	407	174	525
15	41	55	159	95	299	135	404	175	536
16	48	56	129	96	306	136	410	176	526
17	51	57	166	97	307	137	411	177	527
18	52	58	167	98	308	138	412	178	528
19	53	59	173	99	313	139	417	179	529
20	55	60	181	100	323	140	421	180	540
21	54	61	178	101	315	141	424	181	545
22	59	62	200	102	316	142	428	182	497
23	63	63	201	103	327	143	433	183	554
24	56	64	204	104	330	144	437	184	555
25	67	65	205	105	335	145	419	185	557
26	57	66	206	106	331	146	438	186	559
27	73	67	207	107	338	147	443	187	560
28	77	68	218	108	341	148	444	188	561
29	72	69	220	109	339	149	449	189	566
30	82	70	232	110	346	150	453	190	567
31	87	71	233	111	348	151	454	191	563
32	88	72	234	112	349	152	455	192	564
33	86	73	237	113	352	153	456	193	569
34	89	74	238	114	353	154	458	194	577
35	94	75	239	115	371	155	459	195	575
36	90	76	243	116	359	156	460	196	579
37	93	77	244	117	358	157	463	197	582
38	104	78	251	118	361	158	469	198	578
39	109	79	248	119	367	159	479	199	598
40	111	80	261	120	372	160	478	200	587

IND = Mission Praise Individual Volumes,
COMB = Mission Praise COMBINED words edition.

IND	COMB	IND	COMB	IND	COMB	IND	COMB	IND	COMB
201	590	249	712	297	17	345	131	393	229
202	591	250	707	298	23	346	126	394	230
203	599	251	727	299	27	347	127	395	213
204	601	252	715	300	24	348	128	396	231
205	546	253	729	301	32	349	137	397	235
206	602	254	—	302	35	350	130	398	246
207	604	255	730	303	37	351	136	399	247
208	605	256	734	304	34	352	140	400	252
209	613	257	736	305	39	353	147	401	245
210	615	258	738	306	43	354	141	402	250
211	617	259	739	307	44	355	145	403	253
212	624	260	742	308	45	356	152	404	254
213	627	261	744	309	46	357	150	405	256
214	625	262	746	310	47	358	155	406	257
215	631	263	748	311	60	359	156	407	267
216	633	264	753	312	49	360	160	408	268
217	640	265	755	313	58	361	162	409	269
218	641	266	766	314	61	362	168	410	270
219	646	267	762	315	62	363	171	411	276
220	647	268	759	316	64	364	175	412	271
221	649	269	760	317	65	365	177	413	273
222	650	270	765	318	66	366	176	414	280
223	652	271	767	319	68	367	182	415	282
224	655	272	768	320	79	368	183	416	281
225	658	273	778	321	69	369	184	417	289
226	656	274	769	322	74	370	185	418	290
227	660	275	770	323	75	371	187	419	293
228	686	276	779	324	76	372	188	420	294
229	666	277	787	325	80	373	189	421	296
230	674	278	784	326	83	374	194	422	297
231	677	279	790	327	84	375	193	423	298
232	672	280	780	328	91	376	191	424	311
233	678	281	796	329	96	377	198	425	314
234	682	282	402	330	99	378	192	426	317
235	681	283	1	331	100	379	196	427	320
236	684	284	2	332	101	380	195	428	312
237	697	285	5	333	106	381	209	429	322
238	689	286	6	334	108	382	202	430	324
239	691	287	7	335	102	383	203	431	325
240	694	288	8	336	114	384	211	432	259
241	706	289	9	337	112	385	210	433	332
242	696	290	15	338	113	386	212	434	334
243	698	291	10	339	118	387	214	435	329
244	699	292	16	340	122	388	219	436	336
245	701	293	18	341	119	389	224	437	337
246	702	294	19	342	120	390	225	438	340
247	705	295	20	343	123	391	226	439	342
248	708	296	22	344	124	392	227	440	343

IND	COMB	IND	COMB	IND	COMB	IND	COMB	IND	COMB
441	344	489	451	537	552	585	670	633	776
442	345	490	464	538	553	586	661	634	775
443	347	491	457	539	558	587	663	635	781
444	302	492	462	540	562	588	664	636	782
445	350	493	465	541	565	589	669	637	783
446	355	494	472	542	568	590	673	638	785
447	357	495	474	543	572	591	676	639	789
448	360	496	475	544	573	592	679	640	786
449	366	497	477	545	576	593	685	641	793
450	365	498	468	546	570	594	675	642	791
451	364	499	481	547	580	595	687	643	792
452	368	500	483	548	581	596	688	644	795
453	369	501	485	549	583	597	692	645	797
454	373	502	482	550	585	598	648	646	794
455	370	503	498	551	586	599	693	647	798
456	377	504	491	552	588	600	703	648	12
457	376	505	492	553	589	601	704	649	14
458	384	506	493	554	592	602	709	650	28
459	389	507	530	555	593	603	710	651	42
460	391	508	502	556	594	604	711	652	50
461	392	509	503	557	595	605	695	653	92
462	397	510	504	558	597	606	714	654	97
463	398	511	505	559	607	607	716	655	98
464	399	512	507	560	600	608	717	656	95
465	400	513	501	561	603	609	718	657	71
466	409	514	513	562	608	610	719	658	110
467	405	515	514	563	614	611	720	659	121
468	408	516	512	564	610	612	722	660	125
469	413	517	511	565	611	613	723	661	135
470	414	518	516	566	616	614	724	662	134
471	415	519	518	567	618	615	725	663	138
472	416	520	517	568	620	616	726	664	149
473	418	521	520	569	626	617	728	665	157
474	423	522	521	570	622	618	731	666	164
475	426	523	524	571	638	619	732	667	169
476	431	524	533	572	628	620	733	668	174
477	433	525	522	573	629	621	735	669	190
478	434	526	523	574	630	622	740	670	172
479	440	527	532	575	635	623	745	671	199
480	435	528	538	576	636	624	749	672	179
481	430	529	548	577	637	625	752	673	180
482	429	530	539	578	634	626	754	674	208
483	436	531	541	579	639	627	761	675	215
484	441	532	542	580	644	628	758	676	216
485	442	533	544	581	645	629	764	677	217
486	446	534	550	582	651	630	763	678	221
487	447	535	549	583	653	631	771	679	223
488	452	536	551	584	659	632	773	680	241

IND	COMB	IND	COMB	IND	COMB	IND	COMB	IND	COMB
681	240	697	318	713	448	729	547	745	713
682	242	698	321	714	445	730	556	746	665
683	236	699	326	715	432	731	574	747	643
684	222	700	303	716	427	732	571	748	642
685	248	701	351	717	425	733	621	749	747
686	260	702	310	718	403	734	596	750	721
687	255	703	300	719	422	735	619	751	737
688	264	704	363	720	461	736	609	752	741
689	283	705	378	721	466	737	612	753	750
690	291	706	356	722	484	738	606	754	766
691	286	707	387	723	489	739	632	755	772
692	265	708	393	724	534	740	623	756	777
693	292	709	390	725	535	741	654	757	757
694	301	710	354	726	531	742	657	758	788
695	305	711	406	727	508	743	690		
696	309	712	420	728	509	744	671		

TABLE 6

SONGS INCLUDED ONLY IN
MISSION PRAISE COMBINED EDITION

All you that pass by	26
Children of Jerusalem	70
Christ the Way of life	78
Clap your hands, you people all	81
Come and see, come and see	85
Come, watch with us	105
Come, ye faithful, raise the anthem	103
Cradled in a manger	107
Down from his glory	116
For the might of your arm	154
Freely, for the love he bears us	161
Give me a heart	165
Give thanks with a grateful heart	170
I am waiting for the dawning	262
I was sinking deep in sin	450
I'd rather have Jesus	319
Immortal love, for ever full	328
In loving-kindness Jesus came	333
Jesus, I am resting, resting	362
Judge eternal, throned in splendour	395
Lord of all being, throned afar	439
Morning has broken	467
My goal is God himself	470
My God, I thank you	471
My Lord, what love is this	476
Not what these hands have done	487
O Saviour Christ, I now confess	519
On Christmas night all Christians sing	537
Onward Christian soldiers	543
Saviour, again to thy dear name	584
Sweet is the hope	277
The love of Christ who died for me	662
The trumpets sound	667
The world was in darkness	668

HYMNS FOR TODAY'S CHURCH

Jubilate Hymns
Consultant Editor: Rt Rev Michael Baughen

The natural hymn book for use alongside modern Bible translations and modern orders of service. This book combines the best of traditional hymns with modern compositions of proven quality.

Hymns for Today's Church Second Edition is available as music, melody and words only cased, giant print edition cased and words only paperback. The First Edition is still available in music and words cased. Packs are available to churches and schools at reduced prices.

> "Hymns for Today's Church is simply the best on the
> market for use as the Church's basic hymn book.
> The congregation are able to sing the old favourites
> and value very much the wealth of new material."
>
> Rev Robert Key, St Leonard's, Eynsham, Oxford

> "An excellent modern hymnal with traditional hymns and
> modern 'songs'. A good musical companion to the ASB."
>
> Rev W J Moxon, St John the Evangelist, Altrincham

CHURCH FAMILY WORSHIP

Jubilate Hymns

Church Family Worship provides in one volume hymns, songs, prayers and service material suitable for both family worship and for regular use in more informal services. ASB Morning and Evening Prayer and the full text of Holy Communion Rite A is included, together with free church service material.

Church Family Worship is available in music and words cased and words only paperback. Packs are available to churches and schools at reduced prices.

> "I am much impressed by both the material it contains and the way in which it has been presented. It will no doubt prove an enormous asset to those responsible for the leading of family worship."
>
> Robert Runcie, former Archbishop of Canterbury

> "This book may be commended to a worship leader in any church."
>
> Baptist Times